LOVE NEVER FAILS

LOVE
NEVER
FAILS

THE DAILY ROUND AND COMMON TASKS CARING FOR A DISABLED WIFE

DON SNUGGS

Matador
9 Priory Business Park,
Wistow Road, Kibworth Beauchamp,
Leicestershire. LE8 0RX
Tel: 0116 279 2299
Email: books@troubador.co.uk
Web: www.troubador.co.uk/matador
Twitter: @matadorbooks

ISBN 978 1788035 613

British Library Cataloguing in Publication Data.
A catalogue record for this book is available from the British Library.

Printed and bound by CPI Group (UK) Ltd, Croydon, CR0 4YY
Typeset in 11pt Adobe Garamond Pro by Troubador Publishing Ltd, Leicester, UK

Matador is an imprint of Troubador Publishing Ltd

MIX
Paper from
responsible sources
FSC® C013604

Sandie and I dedicate this little book to all those sufferers and carers who day after day and night after night slog at their tasks with hope, love and compassion and, in seeing what we have done, will know they are not alone; there are many like us.

CONTENTS

FOREWORD

As a practising nurse and a carer for over ten years, I fully understand the difficulties, frustrations and joy that come with supporting a relative who has become disabled from a long-term illness.

Through my nursing role and caring for people in the community, I came into contact with a lady who suffered the effects of a neurological progressive condition and who was being cared for by her husband, whom I had known some years ago whilst training as a nurse.

This book is a personal account of a retired registered nurse and acupuncturist, who at the age of seventy-five gets married. In his senior years, he marries a lady who has a progressive condition, is wheelchair dependant, and requires care with all activities of daily living.

This book is about them as a newly married couple; more specifically, it's about an elderly couple who face the challenging task of trying to ensure they are both able to enjoy their time together, but within the confines of disability, illness and available support. The author has written down his feelings, his encounters with carers; a blow-by-blow account of challenges, frustrations, failures and successes. He describes the day-to-day routine and the steely tenacity that is required of a carer. Through his descriptions, he paints a picture of how helping to support his wife have a '*Normal Day*' requires total commitment, attention to detail, and selflessness. He gives an insight into what it is like to be the sole carer and husband to a disabled wife, their daily routine and the role that is a twenty-four hours a day, seven days a week job.

The reader will glimpse an insight into his previous nursing knowledge and how he uses this to understand the importance of *'treating the patient and not just the symptom'*. His perseverance and resolve to do the best for his wife are more than admirable, especially more recently, as they have both been troubled with periods of ill health. Over the ten years that he has cared for his wife, he has come into contact with external support providers in the hope that it would ease his caring role. Sadly, his encounters have not been positive and he gives his opinion on how they could be improved to support others in a similar situation. Despite the enormity of the caring role he took on, he shows with care and love that he is able to give his wife a reasonable life in spite of her condition.

Many carers will relate to his accounts. A read for those who, as carers, will know what the role entails, especially in those lonely, tiresome nights when there is no clocking off… As health care professionals, we have a duty to listen and learn from patients and carers if we are to raise the profile of improving the experience of care. Getting the basics right is essential. It can be the small things that make the difference between a good or poor experience.

Catherine Semple, Registered Nurse

INTRODUCTION

Again and again, we hear of the unacceptable treatment in the care of the helpless and disabled people who suffer from disease or old age. After investigation, the usual platitudes are expressed by those in charge of these patients: "Lessons will be learned." Oh yes, are they? Until the next time, maybe! Being in my eighty-fifth year, I wonder what will happen to me when I am no longer capable! This introduction, or should I say polemic, comprises my personal thoughts about this situation after many years of caring for the sick as a medical professional since 1949, and still in harness!

The understanding of sickness appears to be sadly lacking in those carers who abuse, but they all receive some training, they say. Is it because, in general, many who work outside the NHS are not accountable to a professional body? This can take away their living and prosecute them for failing to achieve the standard required, as is the case of NHS employees who have gone through a rigorous training scheme, and are employed to work to a high standard, and are accountable by law to maintain a 'duty of care' at all times and in all circumstances. In my lifetime, I have seen many of those carers, who get very limited training, sent out to deal with the most vulnerable in society in the patients' own homes, some patients with many complex conditions. However, it is increasingly difficult for care companies to recruit as the carers recruited are only paid the minimum wage; and with a diminishing employment market with higher levels in work, those looking for jobs as carers cannot afford to live on their pay and go elsewhere, so the applicants are what are left when all other jobs are filled. These carers, often taken on and employed having limited education standards, and many who do not speak or write good English, or come from a different culture and generation to their patients, have problems in communicating. I recall working once in deepest East Anglia; to the locals, I was a foreigner as I certainly did not speak their version of English, and confusion sometimes occurred! This fact should not, of course, be a bar to their employment if they are trained properly, or rather taught how to do the job competently, and this costs money. Some do very well, but although many of these carers have been told about the kind of problems they will meet, they have not been told how to deal with the funny ways and quirks that patients have with their presenting condition. For example, it is one thing to know what causes paralysis of a limb, but what do you do, or not do, to ensure that the patient and limb are protected and kept free from further trauma? Or how does an affected patient living alone put toothpaste on a toothbrush if they have the use of only one arm and poor eyesight? But this is often only a mirror of the practice of general medicine, where often, unfortunately, the disease appears to get more attention than the patient who suffers from it.

Unfortunately, in the early '80s when education and advancement of knowledge took over from good old-fashioned hard nursing graft, some government minister, wanting to raise the profile of the nursing profession, felt the best way to ensure this was for all 'trained' nurses to have a degree, and the universities set up courses to do this. Many students who before this time would have started work literally on the shop floor, cleaning the wards and lockers each morning, and performing such 'menial' tasks as serving meals, washing and bathing, emptying bedpans and cleaning up their patients' incontinence, got to know their patients and their problems first hand, by talking and being with them. Instead, they were being given a series of lectures by very clever, knowledgeable people, with not a lot of experience of care, and a few placements on the wards, but not by learning to be in charge of a department coping with both patients and junior staff with all its frustrations, and learning the concept of total accountability. I recall a young friend of ours at a university on a nursing degree course writing a dissertation on 'Nursing care in pre-revolutionary Russia'. Very useful indeed if you are reading history! Unfortunately, this huge vital student workforce had to be replaced, hence the everlasting complaint by the government of the chronic shortage of nurses, so they were replaced with low paid workers of various standards who were supposed to be managed by these graduate nurses, who themselves had never been in the muck and bullets of a desperately busy, overloaded surgical ward. So who lowered the standards? Clever politicians, of course, who thought it a good idea at the time to mess about with things of which they knew little or nothing, and still do so!

So today, in my eighty-fifth year, looking at the still rising complaints in the caring system, I see little change, whilst governments tinker and mess around the edges of the problem, either throwing more and more money at it, or having more, and sometimes less managers as the mood takes them. And still the problem remains; it is the old, and the disabled, and the helpless that bear the brunt of it all, and are lessons learned after another almost foreseeable disaster occurs, or another administration comes to power? As Eliza Doolittle said, "Not bloody likely!"

But ten years ago I left the nursing profession and private practice in which I had worked for nearly sixty years and entered another aspect of care which I never thought would happen to me. I now look after my disabled wife Sandie, and my word, it's a different ball game looking after someone you love dearly!

Caring for a fellow sufferer, particularly on your own, can be a stressful and lonely task, and even when working for an employer, if the carer is not supported, can lead to tiredness and an unnoticed lowering of standards. The old phrase, 'Who cares for the carer?' applies indeed. If they get no moral or physical assistance from whatever source, then it can be like the old song of the Miller of Dee: *I care for nobody, no not I, For nobody cares for me.* I hope I never get to that point, but I've known some who nearly did. Yes, it can be a lonely life.

A friend sent my wife, Sandie, and I a brochure one day when all was collapsing around us and I was going into hospital for surgery and needed someone to care for her until I recovered. Sandie has multiple schlerosis of many years standing and is paraplegic, also with use in only one arm. The brochure had a lovely picture depicting a nicely dressed old gent, sitting in a chair looking out on a well-tended rose garden with all the roses in flower. He looked so content, mainly because a pretty young woman, in an immaculate white uniform with a lovely figure, was offering him a glass of orange juice which he gratefully accepted with a beaming smile. Dear readers, if you are still with me, it ain't like that, believe me! Waiters do that in the best hotels!

So this book is only a series of essays recorded as situations arise as I care for my Sandie. It does not set out to be a textbook on care; some parts are indeed anecdotal, some may raise eyebrows, but it is a portrayal of my feelings by being in the midst of it all, and is often written in the heat of the battle when I am so tired that I wonder where the next burst of energy is going to come from! My blood pressure is fortunately controlled with medication. What would happen were I to run out of pills! No, these are not literate masterpieces. It's my heart talking, not my head, and sometimes as I look back at what has happened to my darling wife, Sandie, in the past years before we were married, my blood pressure goes up, and my heart sinks! No, I repeat: this is not a textbook on the care of the sick, immobile patient. I know all the arguments for and against some of the things I have had to do for her; it's an observation of the daily grind which never ceases day or night, year after year, in which I am involved; but like love, it brings its own rewards.

The title of my observations, for want of a better word, is from St Paul's great polemic in the *New Testament*, possibly the greatest love poem written in the English tongue which begins, *If I speak in the tongue of men and of angels and have not love, I am only a clanging gong or resounding cymbal… If I have the faith that can move mountains but have not love, I am* nothing, etc…

Love is what underpins my care of Sandie, my dear wife. No, the care of a paraplegic patient with progressive MS is not easy; it needs a lot of love. When, as a practitioner, you find yourself with a close family member as a patient with this problem, and although you have been caring for the acutely ill for over sixty years, and then marry this person you love who has a chronic neurological condition needing twenty-four-hour total care, you are proceeding into unknown territory. The psychology in care for the acutely ill and the chronic incurable condition from which the patient suffers are two different things. The practice of care is turned on its head; day becomes night, pain and spasm, bowels, waterworks, catheters and pressure areas take over the conversation along with medication and exercises – often of little help – and the only thing left for you both is hope: hope that tomorrow and the days thereafter will be better than today!

However, I decided to keep not a diary, but this record of the pleasant and unpleasant day-to-day struggles as I care for my dear wife, of random thoughts as they came to me, but also the input from so many people, friends, practitioners, carers, professionals and others, people who see the patient – and then go home to tea and the TV, leaving us to get on with it! Our life is twenty-four hours a day, seven days a week and 365 days a year. I share them all with Sandie who has almost as much trouble as a medical ward full of patients! But somehow we get by. Love never fails!

So for what these notes are worth – and I hope they will help some, and make some realise, both patients and carers, that they are not alone, that there are a lot of people like this in these situations – these disconnected (sometimes) jottings are also a means to relieve a carer's feelings – mine!

CHAPTER 1

AND THIS IS HOW
IT ALL STARTED!

S andie and I were reminiscing the other day as I dressed
her after another visit to the toilet.

"How many times have I done this over the years?"
I asked her.

"Many, many times," she laughingly replied.

She does laugh; in fact, laughs a lot, even at my jokes,
unless she throws something at me instead! And that is one
of the main things which keeps us going, I believe.

After all, I am getting on a bit and finding the repeated
tasks difficult at times, but they are often eased by a laugh,
joke, or some fond reminiscence.

I qualified after a gruelling three-year course in
alternative medicine with a licentiate in acupuncture
whilst still working in an NHS hospital as a nurse tutor
and set up practice in a most suitable house which I
found, I am sure, by good luck. The house had at its side a
consulting room with waiting area and toilet en suite, also
with private access and good parking for those who came
to consult me.

Acupuncture in 1983 was a therapy quite new to the
area, but it was not until 1992 that I was financially secure
and so able to leave the NHS and work for myself from

home. It was very slow-going initially, but as I built up my reputation, the money began to come in.

But it was not one of these way-out therapies offering unbelievable cures that I offered to those who came to see me, who had gained no help from either general medicine or other therapies, or had even been offered certain cure. I was at pains to tell them that cure I could not, but could offer help to them to make their experience of illness more bearable and possibly comfort or relieve them of their distress as suggested by August Pare the 18th century physician, as being the primary role of the practitioner.

I recall one of my first patients who came to see me with severe osteoarthritis of his hip causing him many sleepless nights and an inability to walk more than ten yards because of the pain. "Can you cure me?" he asked.

"No," I replied. "But I can probably relieve some of your pain."

After examining him and telling him his only way to a cure was to have a total hip replacement, he snarled at me, "You're as bad as the rest of them; all they want to do is cut me up," and with that, stormed out, slamming the door behind him. I never saw him again, but some people you cannot help!

That's a good start, I thought, *no success, no fee, no goodwill! But that's life!*

Having spent many years in both the NHS and the RAF medical branch, I was not discouraged by that episode, and this was really one of the reasons I had decided to study alternative medicine because dealing with sick people, always using a medical model, which only concentrates on the disease, I'd almost forgotten that it was a person who had the problem. The patient's experience of the disease is unique and is a choice, not that they are aware of the fact that their reaction to their problem is multifactorial – comprising beliefs, upbringing, education, age, social position, and gender. Pain in loneliness is so much worse when you are on your own, despairing at failure to find relief and having been fed platitudes or "Take these tablets, they will help" and they don't or "Well, what do you expect? After all, you've got A, B or C!" What indeed?

However, the practice became well established, meaning that I was seeing patients from all over the country recommended by word of mouth, not, I think, because of media coverage – all they could talk about was miracles – but because I was honest with what I told patients regarding what I could or could not do for them. Indeed, a lot of what I talked to them about was quite often not only their sickness, but health, lifestyle, cars, mortgages, gardening and the thousand and one things that worried patients and got in the way of their well-being. I was not an expert in any of them, but seeing some twenty patients a day, one did garner quite a knowledge of things that could be passed on.

But to get to the nub of what I am writing about – Sandie came to see me one day in 1988 after some eight years of symptoms of MS on and off, but continually worsening. She could not walk properly or do much but sit in her house and watch it deteriorate around her to her distress. She'd lost control of her life.

Her husband was a very busy professional man who was often away from home and she had spent many weeks either in homes or hospital, or being cared for by the social services. She'd had a variety of treatments, but most agencies had given up as she did not improve with their help. She ended up being seen at the local hospital's pain clinic, but even they could not help her much and the sister in charge, a friend of mine, phoned to ask if I could see her. The consultant could see no way round her problems of continual leg spasm and pain. I agreed to see her the following day, and at 11am she and her husband arrived. She was walking badly with the use of crutches and sat down looking dispirited and exhausted, almost swallowed up in my big Queen Anne armchair in which I liked patients to sit as I interviewed them. She was a pretty, neat, young-looking little woman, forty-one years old, nicely dressed and pale-faced. After the initial introductions, I moved towards her in my office chair and took her hands in mine. They were small, cold and dry. I looked into her eyes. "What is the best thing in your life at present?" I asked her.

"Going to bed at night," she replied quietly.

"And the worst?" I asked.

She thought for a moment, then replied in a small voice, looking hesitantly at her husband sitting beside her, "Waking up and finding I'm still alive." Not much hope there, I thought; a future of no more than twelve hours!

So here was a problem, but that was twenty-eight years ago; she is at this moment sitting in her chair reading her Kindle. So how did we get here, she and I married to each other and sharing jokes together?

How did we get here indeed, married to each other and sharing jokes? A long story… twenty-eight years of success and failure along the way, always trying, never giving up, looking forward, come what may. Yes, that sounds pretty trite, but that was the way it was: initially, me the practitioner trying to help an MS patient; a lonely, despairing one who could see no light at the end of the tunnel. It was there, but pretty dim, and my word, she had to look for it and needed a lot of help to find it. It still glows dimly at times; indeed, it has never gone out, but is still there and we keep it alight together.

And here was I with this small, despairing disabled patient, her life destroyed by disease, misunderstood by family, and with few friends; funny where they all go when trouble strikes! As she lay on my examination couch, I did the usual checks: cold, wasted limbs; painful joints; constipated; depressed; and emotionally labile. Already we'd had a few tears. Most of my questions initially were regarding physical problems. She was reluctant to open up even about those, and I realised as I sat and wrote up her notes, she could not and would not let go with her husband present. He was a man with a strong personality, and could not conceive of the idea of the possibility that he could be one day in the situation where he was totally dependent on another person for his very day-to-day needs, as was his wife at that moment. That was obvious by his replies to the questions I put to him.

The most important approach to her now was to provide comfort and reassurance. I massaged her feet and legs, arms and back and even her hands, head and face, and she visibly began to relax within a short time. I treated her minor problems with acupuncture and she went to sleep. I let her sleep as I wrote up her notes, then woke her up and asked her to come again in a few days and quietly said, "On your own."

She came weekly thereafter; I used the same regime, modified as necessary, each session lasting about an hour, with a lot of words, often a few tears. She came and went by taxi, and slowly she began to improve and live again. It was now within three months before Christmas. I asked her what she would be doing. She told me she had relatives coming and she was already planning the meal, not looking forward only to twelve hours now, but three months! So we were getting somewhere. At least she said she knew somebody at last who had not given up on her care! She was now sleeping better, alimentary function much improved and even walking better with her sticks and looking forward each week to coming to my clinic, and on the whole, was a far happier woman.

After a bit of thought and discussion with my director of nurse education at the hospital where I was teaching nurses, I asked him if I could bring Sandie to a session to help me teach nurses the care of the immobile patient. There are not many chronic sick in general hospitals; they're really for the acutely ill.

He agreed with alacrity. His wife had MS, so he understood. This started a weekly visit to the hospital where, of course, Sandie was the centre of attention for a day, but because I could not get the NHS to pay her I took her out to a local hostelry each week for lunch. This got her back to some sort of normality and got her out of the house. So each week she improved in general health. Her MS, of course, was not improved, but she was experiencing her problems in a better way than heretofore.

One day, she came in to see me with a big smile on her face; she had ventured out to the local shop in her power chair. As she waited to be served, a man leaned over her and asked the assistant for something. She now had the puff to jab him with her elbow and say, "I was here first. Wait your turn!" The man had to apologise! I think that was the best sign yet that she was getting there.

So the weekly sessions with massage and acupuncture, and visits to the classroom and the pub, helped to bring her back from the brink of despair and she was a much happier woman, but then her husband changed jobs and they moved away to Norfolk and I saw no more of her until 2006, and that's the rest of the story!

CHAPTER 2

BACK AGAIN

Sandie and I met again late in 2006 when she called me one Saturday morning to say she was back in Peterborough. We had kept in touch with each other in a desultory way when she lived in Norfolk, me advising both her and her husband as and when required. I had known that she had lost her husband to a nasty malignant disease, and there was little I could do but offer comforting words. But following this episode, she was on her own in a big house cared for by social services or by the few friends she had, not an enviable situation to be in and now little better than the previous fifteen years during which she had spent much time in homes or hospital when her condition worsened, or when her husband was away on business.

It was also a bad time for me. My wife was suffering from a terminal malignant disease which required much nursing care, mainly provided by myself, and eventually in May 2006 she died and left me bereft, still running a practice, but for what? It certainly was not for my welfare, and although it was better working and caring for others so as not to stagnate intellectually, it was tiring, although rewarding professionally.

One day in July, Sandie called me, asking for treatment again. She had returned to Peterborough from Norfolk and bought a small bungalow which had been fitted up with a wet room and other aids. Complaining of the usual things: constipation, tiredness, frustration that she was getting little out of life, and so on, all the usual problems of the immobile patient on her own and reliant on the goodwill of others, which was not always forthcoming. I visited her as she requested in her little bungalow. It was sad to see her state now, desperately lonely and cared for in a less than adequate way, every box ticked indeed, but with the overriding feeling that she was nothing more than another number to be sorted out and was there any future in it? But I found she was still the same sweet person; how she maintained this state I do not know, and now at the age of fifty-eight, trying to not be a nuisance to her few friends and to the medical staff involved must have been more than difficult. If she did complain, nobody seemed to listen to what she said, or misunderstood her, but what she did not say was the most important thing, and they needed to make time to do this, and time, they always complained, was a commodity in short supply, so they didn't bother.

I visited her over the next few weeks and she began to look forward to my calls, again the usual problems of the immobile patient, and although she was up in her power chair, her sphere of influence ended at her fingertips, but I could never meet all her wants. Her needs could be coped with, but I did my best and we often had a few tears as I left. I had work to fill my time, but for her, reading and switching on the TV was the extent of her abilities. It was unfulfilling, to say the least. I realised, however, that she was becoming dependent on me, and tried to think of a better life for her, contemplating hospice care and live-in carers.

What could I do for this young-at-heart paraplegic patient of mine? But there seemed to be no answer. Surely there was something better? But I did find the answer, and it came out of the blue.

One evening, after a busy day in my practice, I relaxed for a while in my back garden. It was a lovely autumn evening; the sun was just setting, the only sounds were those of traffic on the main road a quarter of a mile away and some birdsong, when the line of a hymn I'd heard in my childhood came to me: *Thy way not mine oh Lord, however hard it be.* I shook myself and got up, went indoors, found my copy of *Hymns Ancient and Modern* and read the rest of the poem, went to bed with it on my mind using it as a prayer and awoke next morning after a good night's sleep. As I opened my eyes, the answer came to me: of course, marry her. I did love her and believed she loved me! I went straight down to her bungalow, and on my knees asked her to marry me, and she did not refuse. She said later had I not asked she would have asked me! And so we had to devise a blueprint that would direct us in the new future for both of us, and the blueprint was designed essentially around love, and so we got to work on it.

That day in June when we were married on my seventy-fifth birthday, was one of the happiest days of our new life. Not, of course, without its bizarre moments: at the reception as we cut the cake together, it skidded off the table to the horror of the assembled company and hit the floor with a thud. It says something for the quality of the baking that it neither damaged the floor nor broke up as it hit the carpet! The maker of the cake – a friend – remarked later that she had obviously put too little butter into its creation and when the following day I threw out on the garden what was left, even the birds did not find it all that palatable and it stayed on the path for a week before the birds eventually devoured it peck by peck! Was this some omen for our life together?

The months leading up to our great day were not without their traumas. Sandie's bungalow was too small for all our gear, so we decided to have an extension built. It was to be a large one and I asked my son-in-law, a jobbing builder, if he would do the honours and build to our specification, which, bless him, with the design of the architect and other outsourced workers and tradesmen, he did to a very high standard. But we made the mistake of failing to heed all advice, and the cushion floor laid in the dining area, the underlying concrete being incompletely dry, rose up in places as if to meet its maker in the great blue yonder. However, a lesson learned: listen to the experts; and the extension was completed properly the day before the wedding, which pleased us greatly.

Two weeks before the ceremony, we had a practice run at the parish church. As we went through the procedure, at the appropriate moment I was directed to take Sandie's hand in mine, which I did, to be asked by the curate why I was taking Sandie's pulse, for heaven's sake, little realising what I was doing. In the emotion of the moment I had reverted to my clinical practice in taking her pulse! However, all went well with the rehearsal. I asked that the service could be conducted with us all sitting, apart from the curate, so we were all at Sandie's level in her wheelchair, but the congregation was asked to stand for the final blessing at the end of the ceremony - apart from Sandie of course.

So with all the planning, sorted out, what could go wrong? Indeed, what could? By now, I had sold my practice and prepared to move in with Sandie a few days before the wedding to help her get ready. But as I would have to have slept in a z-bed in Sandie's room, with her towering above me in her hospital bed, we decided to get double electric adjustable beds and purchased a unit from the shop to be delivered when we were away on honeymoon. One morning, before I came down to the bungalow, I found her in great distress. She was still on her own at night, of course. Her carers would not arrive until about 7 am. She had got into a muddle in the middle of the night when her legs went into total spasm and somehow got trapped in the mechanism of the bed, threatening to do her harm. She pressed her call medallion and asked for help. The person on the end of the line promptly called the ambulance for the attendants to unravel her. They had arrived at 4 am and shouted at her for wasting their time. They were not there, they said, for her comfort and had better things to do. Why couldn't she wait until 7 when the carers came? This resulted in me contacting the principal ambulance officer; there was a bruising phone call – for her, not me – regarding an unacceptable and disgraceful bad-mannered response by her staff, and eventually an apology was forthcoming.

So we had our ups and downs, but Sandie now had a friend at court to speak up for her, more than a friend, I hope, and on June 2nd we became one!

CHAPTER 3

THOUGHTS ON THE PAST

Our marriage in June 2007 on my seventy-fifth birthday went well: a lovely, happy day, sunny and in the beautiful parish church of St John's, Yaxley, but more of that later. Suffice it to say, the learning curve got a lot steeper from that day onwards.

Sandie is unique in my experience. She does not complain and she is sweet and undemanding. These are not the only two characteristics she has that I love; she has plenty more, and one would have thought they would have stood her in good stead with her sickness in the past. But she is a paraplegic with only one hand she can use, so is therefore unable to change her position in bed or in her power chair to even improve her comfort without help. Use of any utilities on her own outside or in the home is beyond her capability; but for all that, she now lives a good and rewarding life, so long as she is allowed to, and it is my pleasure to let her, in spite of everything.

The only two things she can do to exercise some control in her life are to change her location or use her tongue! So Sandie actually has little control of her world beyond the confines of her chair. But to change her location she needs her power chair, so long as people get out of her way, and as long as there are no kerbs to mount, the pathways are wide enough, the doors open to touch, there is enough light to see where she is going and no dangerous hills or gullies and so on – a hundred things to get in the way, unnoticed by the able walker. Her other control is her tongue. True, she can ask for what she wants but needs have to be supplied by others. But if she articulates her needs, she needs to be heard, and if people are too busy to listen or do not understand, or misunderstand what she says, or it is inconvenient for them at the time, then life ceases to be life, and becomes an existence.

Yes, all of this I had to learn, even though I had been caring for the acutely ill for years. This was a different world I was entering! This is the problem of caring for the chronically ill in an acute situation.

So how does she cope? She has had a long history of MS since 1984 and has been cared for by carers, local authority homes, hospitals and places and situations too numerate to mention. Now she lives with me; I thought I knew it all until I lived with her! I fulfil all her needs and love doing it. I provide her wants as far as is practicable and possible, but unlike others in all I do, I try not to invade her private space, or what little she has. Private spaces in public service sources are given little consideration. "No, we don't like you to close the toilet door when you are in it. You might fall and we would not see," a well-meaning carer said in one home she was in, but would those who say that go to the toilet in a public place themselves and have the door open? That doesn't sound a lot, but to Sandie it was horrible. Does the carer ever get into trouble with a loaded constipated bowel, but can clear it in privacy when the door is shut and nobody is trying to hurry her? Sandie couldn't do this, she tells me, and I have to cope with that problem. She has, as have a lot of MS patients, an automatic bowel with no sphincter control, and when she needs to empty her bowel, she has to do it there and then; very inconvenient for the carer, devastating for the poor patient if nobody will take her to the toilet for whatever reason. Or again, be put back to bed if she cannot go on their demand. "Just wait until after dinner," they say, but she can't, and the carer has even more to clear up when her gut does decide to work, leaving her feeling like a naughty child. I wonder what a carer would say if her boss told her not to go to the toilet in his time, but wait until she went off duty. Grounds for industrial tribunals, no doubt, with a lot of nonsense about human rights! The end result of all that was that Sandie was a troublemaker. Troublemakers are ignored! What would the carer say if she stood in the queue at Starbucks waiting for a cup of coffee to get her through the day and was ignored whilst the server chatted on his mobile phone to his girlfriend? Being ignored is an affront to human dignity.

Yes, this has happened and I am well aware of these situations. She's told me a lot which makes me ashamed of my profession, and a thousand other nasty things which demean the disabled when the response has often been, "Haven't we got enough to do?" said in a petulant tone as though admonishing a naughty child. Do they soothe the patient with, "Well, these things do happen"? No, it's usually "Why didn't you ask?" The answer is obvious: had she asked, she'd have been ignored or misunderstood as there is so little time in a day to do all these things. Yes, time needs managing. She recalls asking for a change of position in bed at 3 in the morning when in an expensive nursing home, to be admonished by the staff that she would have to wait because the particular staff member was doing her monthly returns. She never got that change of position and spent a most uncomfortable night instead. It was obviously inconvenient for that staff member to do her job, failing to appreciate that she worked there for the patient's convenience, and not her own.

No, hold on; I said earlier that Sandie is sweet and undemanding and she knows her carers are busy, but didn't want the brush-off so kept quiet. Neither did they listen to what she didn't say, did they? "So it's okay for you, you're retired," I hear somebody say. Well, try and look after somebody totally dependent on you, and look after yourself at the same time – remember you are totally dependent on yourself as well – and look after a home, with its cooking, housework, shopping, washing of clothes, ironing, maintenance, and all the thousand and one things needed to keep body and soul together for two elderly people. Think of the number of times in a day you go to the toilet, probably four or five times; each time takes you no more than five minutes. I have to organise a trip to the toilet for Sandie and each time can take up to thirty minutes. And I have to go as well! So I organise my time. Time is a management tool always in short supply, but time needs managing like all other bits and pieces in an industry, and is no less important in the care of the sick, in which occupation you never know what will happen next, and usually does!

And often it is the wrong unthinking word or expression which upsets the apple cart. An elderly patient of mine many years ago lost his sight following a stroke. He could still walk but was clumsy. He cannoned into his wife one day who shouted at him, "Look where you're going, man." He was, to say the least, devastated by that remark.

I recall when the theatre trolley arrived to take Sandie to theatre for a small operation, the nurse said, "Come on, hop on the trolley." This hardly gave her confidence in the set-up that they did not know she could not 'hop'!

Yes, I've learned all this and more, I'm afraid, but let me get on with the story and put some of it into context.

CHAPTER 4

WE WED ON MY BIRTHDAY

A lovely day, a lovely marriage ceremony taken by Lucy our curate: a very acceptable curate for any parish. I believe she has gone on to higher things in the administration of the Church of England and deserves to get on! What was so nice about her sermon after the marriage itself was her insight into the problems Sandie and I were going to experience in our new lives, and she spoke very lovingly of the contribution made to our lives in the past by our previous spouses, naming them both. She foresaw the many difficulties we were going to experience in our new situation, offering comfort, advice, prayers and best wishes.

So the ceremony and reception came and went, much laughter and merriment, and much drawing of breath as the wedding cake hit the floor as I have told before, then down to our newly furnished and re-equipped bungalow, all fitted out with the facilities needed for life as an invalid with someone to care for her. It was a marvellous afternoon, surrounded by friends and well-wishers. It went so quickly and it was soon time for me to get Sandie ready for bed. Quite a complex task in a new property, a bit complex even now when through illness I have had to hand over Sandie's care to others until I can get back in harness, and the carers have to find their way around such a different home to their own, irrespective of how much 'training' they say they have been given!

We didn't need any presents to add to our accumulated goodies in combining the best of two homes, so we asked that in lieu, our guests should make a donation to either the Multiple Sclerosis Society or that superb system run by the local hospital called 'Hospital at Home', and both organisations profited well from the generosity of our guests and many friends.

Now Sandie is not keen on holidays. In the past, she has often been to hotels at home and abroad and now objects to being seen to be 'different' from other guests. I therefore found and hired an old farm cowshed, modernised and turned into a wonderful one-level holiday home fitted out for disabled guests, with hoists and wet room and so on for the first part of our honeymoon, not too far away in the Peak District from where we were able to visit local attractions such as Dovedale and the Crich Tramway Museum, each evening returning to our holiday retreat, Cowslip, as it was called (and I dubbed it Cowpat to Sandie's disgust!). As she said, "Men are disgusting!" However, we had a lovely, quiet week together learning a lot about our individual funny ways. Without her knowledge, I had enquired of Thomas Cook about a cruise suitable for persons wheelchair bound with all the necessary facilities for Sandie. They were most helpful and I booked a week's cruise on *Saga Rose*, an ex-Cunarder ship of some 26,000 tons for the week for a cruise to the fiords of Norway. Sandie was a little apprehensive at the prospect, but I persuaded her that it would be the holiday of a lifetime, and so it turned out to be. The crew looked after us wonderfully and it all came up to our expectations. Mealtimes were some of the most interesting times. Not only was the food superb, but in the company of other guests it was wonderfully refreshing to meet such a diverse group of mainly mature professional people in such a friendly atmosphere. We were also able to make a number of onshore visits to places and sites of interest suitable for wheelchair users, and then after a fascinating week, well-looked-after and well-fed, we were met by the Saga minibus at Southampton on return, and within four hours were back at our bungalow again, with many pleasant memories.

But the memories faded rapidly two days after our return. One evening, as I had got Sandie ready for bed – a good half-hour task – and then, as I was getting ready myself, I became confused, unaware of where I was, talking gibberish. Sandie told me afterwards that she thought I'd had a stroke, but the next thing I can recall was waking up in A&E and being treated for pneumonia. The week's luxury in an air-conditioned atmosphere had taken its toll. I must have picked up the bug on board, but given a bag of antibiotics, was sent home the next day to recover, to Sandie's relief!

By this time, however, I was planning to take over all of Sandie's care from social services who had done a reasonable job, no frills, just basics, and I had decided that our sleeping arrangements – she in her hospital bed and me in a z-bed – were unacceptable for a loving married couple, and we had to purchase two adjoining adjustable single beds which had electrical adjusters. These were very comfortable and I was able to deal with Sandie's washing and dressing requirements with ease. However, the care assistants were still doing the occasional stint to allow me to do other things, and housework had to be done. But they complained that the beds were too low and were giving them backaches, so the senior social worker with her entourage arrived one morning and started to complain on their behalf quoting the Health and Safety Act to make their point. So I made my point by asking them which part of the act, one two or three, or which subsection? That floored them and brought the conversation to a stop when I pointed out that this was a subject I'd lectured on at hospital. "Don't come that one with me; and if two healthy young women who would not think twice about climbing a mountain on holiday couldn't do it, why could I at the age of seventy-five?" There was no answer to that, but I did eventually agree to have two bed risers fitted which raised the bed by one and a half inches – I failed to see any difference, and they went away mumbling to themselves! The Health and Safety Act is a good bit of legislation, but when used by the lawyers and the workshy, its usefulness is often destroyed, in my experience.

Did I realise that June day in 2007 the battles I would have to fight in the future, as well as health ones? No, I just went forward with my faith and the assurance that it would work out for the best, and so far it has! I don't think I've made any enemies, but I have certainly raised a few eyebrows by plain speaking when necessary! But what happened next? Read on!

CHAPTER 5

WHEELCHAIRS

I t's funny how life gets complicated with 'things'. People are difficult enough at times, but 'things' can really get in the way.

Our life together has at times been dominated by power chairs and all their works, some good, some bad, some efficient, and some useless and dangerous; but after a lot of experience we now have a couple that suit us well, and that is the whole point: they've got to suit the user no matter how clever or expensive – or inexpensive – they are. One size does not fit all, no matter what the adverts say when they promise jam tomorrow!

But some are useless to the user because they have not been properly researched and the ads have been believed! When we got married, Sandie had one that was only useful in the house and as she did not go out, or want to, it was satisfactory. It couldn't be used in the garden because the garden was not paved at the time, but she had been told by a friend about a marvellous all-singing, all-dancing one that could be used in 99% of circumstances and about the only thing it could not do was to make a cup of tea – according to the brochure! She was most impressed and ordered one and sent off a huge cheque for £10,000 and this monster machine arrived one day, delivered by a white van man who knew nothing about it, dumped it inside the front door, and then disappeared into the great blue yonder! It was not until we had returned from our cruise and I decided to get the car modified with a swivel seat for Sandie, and the back of the car adapted to take a power chair, that I inspected this machine. Somehow a friend had managed to get the contraption into the spare room. Had she ever used it? I asked Sandie. "No, but the cleaner tried it out and she could only get it into the lounge by driving it backwards and then it would only just go through the door," she replied. Not a lot of help for a patient with MS with only one functioning arm and poor eyesight. After a lot of bad-tempered phone calls and threats of legal action quoting the Trade Descriptions Act, some six months later I managed to get most of her money back.

Our next wheelchair disaster resulted in Sandie falling headfirst into a pile of dog poo with the chair on top of her! I had seen the chair in a disabled equipment shop one day. It was designed to take to pieces to transport in the boot of the car; it was cheap and looked just right for casual shopping. It had two big wheels at the back and two small ones at the front, the seat was easily removed and the main frame collapsed into a small size. Ideal, I thought. We tried it out in the garden which by now we had paved, and it worked well, came to pieces easily and reassembled in minutes. It looked a good piece of kit, but her main weight was over the front wheels and they were small. One day in the Tesco car park, having got Sandie comfortable in her chair, I turned to get the shopping bags out of the boot and heard a crash. She had moved forward and the two small wheels had caught in a join in the paving and it tipped over, depositing her face down in a pile of poo with the chair on top of her! This resulted in a call to the GP and a day in bed to recover – after a good wash!

And so we continued to learn and eventually found a chair that suited her, so we bought two. The spare one proved useful for me after some spinal surgery.

But we had another fright with the one which replaced the previous chair. It had some wires showing at the hand control. I wrote to the makers telling them that this was a hazard, and they replied that 'Safety is always paramount in our minds when making chairs'. That was all. So, just before I managed to secure these wires, with Sandie on board going into another store, the wires caught in a shopping trolley, the chair spun round and headed for a plate glass window. I just managed to get it back in control before it smashed into the window. I was so annoyed that the makers took the matter so lightly that I contacted Trading Standards. However, their response was, "Well, it didn't happen and you only had one incident."

Incensed, I snapped back, "The Titanic only sank once; what do you say about that?"

All the manager could say was, "Well, I suppose you are right," and then decided to do something about it.

Some years ago, a friend of mine who had an engineering degree and worked for a major company as a designer of luxury cars, had a crisis of conscience. He decided he should be more worthwhile employed working on medical aids and took a post with a firm making power chairs and wheelchairs for the disabled. He lasted with them a month, finding that their ethos was not about making things for sick disabled persons, but about making a profit, no different in essence to the car company, and so long as they sold, the company was happy.

So my advice to anybody contemplating buying a power chair is to try it out, not just in the showroom but on the paths and roads if you can. Don't listen too much to the salesmen; ask your specialist nurse for advice. The brochures often tell only half the tale. Don't forget, most salesmen are able-bodied, and may think they know all about it, but you are the expert and have a different view of life to them. Listen to what your brain tells you in preference.

But getting the virtually immobile patient ready to go out in the wheelchair is a science on its own! But she does need to see the outside world occasionally. This is done either when the patient is up and dressed, or in bed and awaiting the call to get up! It takes a lot of fiddling around, in particular if the patient is like Sandie and unable to do any useful thing to help, and before a jaunt out to see the sights or whatever, it takes a long time, particularly in winter when a lot of clothes are needed. But when you have got this jumble of arms and legs sorted out and clothed and hoisted into the wheelchair, then there is the fun of getting her in the wheelchair, out of the door and into the car, all requirements needing considerable skill and patience. And just as you are ready, the need, even after you have been assured that all is well and they are comfortable, "Can you empty my bag or can you get me to the toilet?" as the movement has got the otherwise reluctant gut working! "Oh, and have you got the tissues and what about my drinking flask?" And so it goes on, half an hour at the very least. Often longer, believe me. So preparation is the watchword! Then when you get to your destination, reverse the process, go and do your thing, whatever it is, then back into the car, strap her in, make sure all is secure and then come home and repeat the whole operation again when you arrive, and then it's time for lunch which you prepared before you went out if you had the time. So that's the morning gone! But for all that, it is good to get out of the house. Then eat, wash up, clean teeth, etc., lay down on the bed after getting her into the hoist out of the chair – not an easy process – onto the bed and a few moments of inactivity for the carer until it's time to get up again, into the hoist, onto the chair, "Cup of tea?"

"No, have you got any so-and-so? And I want to go to the toilet again, and my bag is full by the way, didn't you notice! What's for tea anyway?" So that's today gone! I'm too shattered to do much more, but more has to be done, and with a smile!

"Good heavens; look at the time. It's nearly bedtime!" Here we go again, but no wheelchair this time after you have got her out of it, parked it, oh yes, and plugged it into the charger, and checked it is okay, and cleared up the dog poo off the carpet that you hadn't noticed when you came in, that was adhering to the wheels of the chair like superglue. *That's still there, I forgot that! Will have to do that before bed! My word, this is the life!* But what's the alternative, cabin fever? How many times did I have to tell nurses, if there is something to do, do it now or you will have two things to do next time!

CHAPTER 6

FILLING TIME

I had never really thought about it before now, but I was now faced with a different sort of patient: Sandie. In this case, it was not a question of just a patient/practitioner relationship, but of two people who loved each other, so the many wants and needs of both are different, but are met in an atmosphere of love!

Many times I have told nurses – and practitioners – that they may well go off duty when their job is done, but the patient is still there. They don't go off duty, so how do they fill their time until the next visit? So what does one do when their immediate needs are met?

Those who have retained all their cognitive skills can indulge themselves in activities such as writing. Others who still have their manual dexterity unimpaired by the condition can knit or sew or paint, for example. But those like Sandie, who has only the use of one arm and whose eyesight is impaired, are limited in what they can do to pass the time. Sandie cannot cook or tidy up around her and has to watch me with my scruffy habits ruin her home!

So the world can look a bleak place, but there are many things we have found to enjoy. I bought a Kindle for her some years ago. She has worn out one and is now on to her second one, and has mastered its funny ways. She has read a lot of books to which she had no access before, unless she could visit the library, and that is too much hard work. With Kindle, at the movement of her hand, she has a whole library at her fingertips. She enjoys this as it takes her away from the mundane world of getting comfortable, coping with the loo, etc. as necessary; it is also useful in that its font can be changed to suit her optical needs. Some things we can do together, and some she does quietly on her own. She has her favourite TV and radio programmes, but her favourite occupation indoors is using her Kindle. I can't admit to liking her choice of reading, but it gets her into the realms of imagination unlike the TV, which is so 'in your face'.

Another source of great enjoyment is in the garden.

We had the garden paved around the flowerbeds some little time ago to allow her to safely use her power chair. With her long-handled trowel and fork, she digs around in the flowerbeds to her heart's content, repairing the havoc created by our resident grey squirrels, but it is the birds which give her the greatest pleasure. We have various feeding stations and bird baths strategically placed. Most are squirrel-proof but you can never beat these creatures. Sandie's favourites are the sparrows, particularly in the spring when they bring their newly fledged youngsters to colonise the garden. The starlings, the most fecund of birds, arrive with their young, overloading all the facilities we have for them, and it is great fun watching the clamour of the young families as they fight for the food and access to the water points. You can almost hear them clamouring to be fed on the suet treats Sandie puts out for them:

"Mum, can I have some?"

"Mum, he's got more than me."

"Mum, can I have some more?"

And the parent birds telling them to "Shut up and wait your turn and wipe your beaks; you look a mess, and don't behave like that. Wait until your father comes home and I tell him."

"George, don't do that to your sister. It's not nice."

"Henry, don't talk with your beak full," and so on! Then the jostling for position to be first in the bird bath. "Will you be patient," mum shouts. "There's only room for five at a time." Oh, what a lot of energy expended! And how Sandie enjoys watching it! Down comes the magpie, a cunning, somewhat ungainly bird is he, picks up a crumb and then in a flash is gone. But then the blackbird, always with us no matter what season, he will eat virtually anything and sometimes cheekily knocks on the window for his ration. The ring doves appear whenever the door opens. They clear up from the sparrows; sparrows are messy feeders and spill half their grain on the path to the delight of the doves and wandering wood pigeons, but the poor little dunnock hardly gets a look in, but patiently scrabbles around under the bushes for some morsel dropped by the other birds.

Then the bird we both love, the little goldfinch, comes for his feast of Niger seeds. They often fly in flocks and on one memorable occasion, ten of the little chaps were lined up on the shed roof waiting their turn to get to the feeder which only accommodates two at a time. Pretty little birds which we always look forward to seeing. And then last, but by no means least, the squirrels cavorting, eating everything in sight, followed by the daily visit of the fox. This year's one is obviously a young one as it is less mangy than last year's, but he eats his fill and is suddenly gone. He moves so very silently and quickly indeed, back to his tramping grounds in the far-off fields. We even have a little wood mouse that lives under the shed and graces us with a visit from time to time, not forgetting the hedgehog, scuttling around and turning the security light on at night.

So we have a virtual menagerie in the garden, and with the water feature I bought Sandie two years ago, now loaded with snails, slugs and the frog, resident at all times, there is no need to be lonely. "Why go to the zoo with all this wildlife around," she said laughingly, "which also includes you!" I know just what she means! But the most welcome but rare visitor indeed is the fox, welcome because he eats the scrapings from our dinner plates and often Sandie leaves a bit for him, but rarely if ever do we see him unless he triggers the security light after dark and we are quick enough to get to the window. But the first time he came was in daylight; maybe he was just casing the joint! A friend of ours, knowing our pleasure in seeing him, brought us a number of meat bones from two joints she had cooked. We put them out as it went dark, but we saw nothing. But the next morning they were gone, so it could only have been the fox as they were too big for our other visitors, the cats, birds and mice, and so on, to carry away. What next? I did see a muntjak deer in the street one day, but only once, and Sandie missed it, unfortunately.

CHAPTER 7

THE CONCEPT OF COMFORT

"Are you sitting comfortably?" asked the TV announcer of the children's programme, "Then I'll begin"… Yes, indeed, if you need to contemplate the finer things of life, undisturbed by pain or some other irritation, comfort is essential. Getting Sandie comfortable is an everlasting requirement to allow her to enjoy her life within the distractions of a chronic illness, so far as it is possible. Maslow in his *Hierarchy of Needs* comes close to this with the section on safety and security. It is a constant source of wonder to me why so many who care for others, in whatever capacity, seem to give the concept of comfort a very low priority when there is a need for treatment. Indeed, many treatments are more effective if the patient is comfortable in as many aspects as possible! Certainly, analgesics are more powerful tools to ease mild to moderate pain if the patient is confident, i.e. comfortable with the idea that the professional knows what they are doing! Many patients have remarked to me, when I have asked about their drug regime, that the GP, or consultant, or nurse, didn't seem to appreciate his or her problem when they were consulted, complaining, "He knows I can't swallow those big tablets" or "I didn't feel comfortable with him as a doctor". Or "I've had those before and they didn't work then!" or "Those tablets are a different colour to the ones

I usually have" and no explanation having been given. And indeed, most professionals rank the concept of comfort as a very low priority when thinking about the patient's treatment, for which, of course, the patient is consulting them. Then the thoughtless question asked when she has to be examined on an examination couch: "Can you stand?"

"No," say I, if I am with her. "She's paraplegic," then the blank embarrassed look. And this from both professional and ancillary staff at times is distressing to say the least.

The concept of comfort is not just about physical things. The idea that a patient in bed with ten pillows should be more comfortable than one with two or no pillows is wrong. You can be comfortable lying on the floor if necessary, but comfort has too many components: physical, emotional, psychological, mental, spiritual, and so on, to be comfortable with oneself as in Maslow's self-actualisation, even when other distracters do exist, being in pain or lonely for example. It is the wonder of the human mind that it can work out that *In whatever state I find myself, therewithal to be content*, and the man who felt that, was in prison and awaiting execution. Indeed, it does sometimes happen that patients delude themselves in spite of their perceived condition.

Sandie is comfortable with the way we do things together to get her as comfortable as we can, and we have worked it out, making sure that all her needs and wants are met so far as is possible, and generally we achieve the goal. When I ask her if she is all right, usually she says, "I'm fine!" and she knows because of my knowledge of her, that if she is, for all the reassurances, not 'fine', she is aware that I am listening not only to what she says, but what she does not say, and believes I can solve the presenting problem immediately – with a bit of luck! There's comfort in that she knows I can help her.

But Sandie became very ill one day with a severe infection and was admitted to hospital for some nine days, of which time she remembers little. But I was concerned enough to be with her most of each day to support her for her stay. The hospital pulled out all the stops for her; she was in the right sort of bed, had enough pillows, sheets and blankets, had a call bell and a hand-held device to change the configuration of the bed, and the bed was fitted with a cot side. All eventualities were covered, except her access to drinking water and food, as her meals were placed on the left side of her bed, the side of her paralysed arm. The cot sides, hardly necessary for a patient unable to move anything but her right arm, were raised, so that when the bed table was eventually placed correctly, she still could not reach over them to get her water and meals. The call bell was on her bad side, all easily remedied, but I had to change it all so she could have some control of her space. She was in a lovely room, in a lovely modern hospital, but the door was always shut. The room overlooked pleasant countryside, but she was not in the position where she could see out. So, were all her needs met? Yes, to a certain extent, but she had little, if any, control of her space even though she was ill. However, as she was not aware all the time of what was happening, I had to think and speak for her. The contribution of the staff, quite rightly, as they saw it, was to keep her clean, warm, well clothed and fed, safe with adequate and secure sanitary arrangements and her treatment provided regularly and expertly. Yes, she did get over the problem, but she was lonely, uncomfortably lonely. She saw the staff when some duty, such as attention to her drips or medicines, was needed. The door of the room remained shut and the cot sides up, in other word, a kind of prison. So, were her needs met? Yes, but not her wants! And if anyone reads this that has been very ill, they'll know the things she, as a chronically ill patient, experienced. Don't forget: when you are ill, you are still the centre of your universe but have lost the power to control anything. Even your fears and aspirations are different and insecurity takes over, and if this is not, or deliberately not, recognised by those caring for you, they are virtually saying, "I'm all right, Jack. Blow your horrible luck." And when, for example, you are gasping for such a simple thing as a cup of tea, to be told, "Not teatime yet," knowing how simple a request this is, or "Can I have the door open?" and so on, to be met with an unqualified denial or not listened to, nor acted upon, the usual reason being lack of time, it is demeaning to somebody who has lost so much control of their life already.

So when the immobile patient finds herself in this position and needs others to take over until she recovers her own ability to take back control insofar as she can, above all, she needs to feel comfortable with her carers, and trust them to want to do the correct thing. Yes, it is hard to satisfy all the demands of the sick. The needs are easy; that is like looking after battery hens, but it's the wants – emotional, spiritual, physical, social, and psychological – that are more difficult to satisfy. St Paul's great polemic on love… *and the greatest of these is love,* says it all. You love yourself; give some of that to those you care for, or do unto others, etc. etc. Then the carer, if willing to do that, is then ready to care for the sick.

Yes, Sandie did get better, but it was a long, hard road. True, she had travelled this one before, but with my love and the correct antibiotics, I was able to get her back to some sort of normality where she smiles again.

From time to time, it is necessary for Sandie to be cared for at home in either my absence, or due to my occasional disability. It is a constant source of wonderment to me why some people choose to be 'carers'. Most say it is because they feel called to care for the sick, and claim by their experience that they have a good knowledge of the problem of the disease the patient has, this knowledge gained from their knowledge of others suffering from the same stated condition. Or they have been told this on their initiation into their post. What they do not seem to be told is that all patients have a different response to their fellow sufferers, even with the same diagnosis. They are not employed to treat the patient's disease or condition, but to help the sufferer to cope with it. But by and large, they do not have the resources, or the wit, to read up on the many ways one can make a patient more satisfied with their state, and experience their problems in a different and better way. The concept that one size fits all is apparently the most prevalent belief; this is what you do in the presenting patient's condition and will do for all who present with the same problem, but with little knowledge as to how, why, when, when not, and so on, to do certain things. Sandie has a paralysed left arm and shoulder muscles, and I am everlastingly telling the carers not to pull her forward with this arm, in case her shoulder dislocates as she has not the muscle power to hold the joint together adequately, and to put her top on over the head first, then the arms, starting with the weak one first. I think the problem is that most are 'trained', if that is the right word, by practising on each other, usually fit, healthy young men and women who are aware of their surroundings, who are fully cognitive of what is going on, and will soon say if such an action hurts, and not the whining, pain-filled, confused patient in old age who will moan if a mosquito lands on their pyjama jacket or is incontinent and ashamed of it, and is always thirsty, and wants to be left alone in all probability, or have some company or be sympathetically listened to. The idea that medicine and medical treatment is the way to ease their burden is erroneous, but is the common opinion of the general public and those uneducated in nursing matters. 'How would I like that done to me?' is a question most need to ask, and don't. Also, the concept of lifestyle is rarely thought about, but it is the way we choose to survive that dictates our health or lack of, and our response to pathogens – that is disease-creating organisms – which take hold in tiredness, malnutrition, unhappiness, etc. and this lifestyle can be modified according to the situation. But that needs flexibility of thought: a commodity I have found to be in short supply among the carers. Some are very good and perceptive, but I would venture to say they are in the minority.

This was well illustrated when knowing that my background was in pain relief among other activities, a carer once asked me what could be done for his twenty-five–year-old daughter who had a severe neuromuscular condition giving her constant pain. I asked him for details and told him that in my opinion there would appear to be little for this lady's condition apart from NSAI drugs or steroids and a change of lifestyle. He replied, "My daughter won't take steroids because they make you fat," and he was of the same opinion. I told him that steroids don't make you fat, but can give you a sense of well-being as the pain is relieved, so one eats more as the stomach empties more quickly, but it requires discipline to control one's eating habits. The young woman in question had two young children, was a single mother, had a busy job, and enjoyed an active social life. Had she ever considered a change of lifestyle? No, it would be too difficult, "She would not be able 'to enjoy herself'," I was told. With a change of lifestyle and the drugs, she had a chance of living better even with some pain. He said his daughter had seen a number of GPs and had been prescribed the appropriate medication for the condition. I doubt this, or she would have been referred for consultant opinion, but had also tried 'various things!' and bought 'stuff' off the Internet. So there was little hope of a resolution to her problem as all factors were against it. When I told the man this, he still replied, "Yes, but I still think that steroids make you fat!" Not much flexibility of thought there, even when the problem was explained. Maybe I did not do it very well!

Sandie's lifestyle had to be changed when we married. I saw to this as a matter of urgency: sleeping times, position in bed, rest times, diet, supplements to her diet, marked attention to bowel and bladder habits, and in an atmosphere of love and enthusiasm and change as necessary. I knew that this would make a difference – and it did. The old pessimism lifted, appetite increased, sleep patterns improved, so she was now experiencing her condition to be more comfortable, reassured that I knew what I was doing because as I explained previously, she was now comfortable with her carer; and because I had taken the trouble to look up and ask questions. It's all online today, irrespective of what I already knew about her condition, and I modify my response to her according to how she feels. No, her MS state has not improved; the damage is done, but it worries her less, and she now lives a much fuller life, and our main comfort, for both of us is that we are together and share everything as one. Our home is part of us, and we are part of it, our familiar surroundings which we love and look after. To describe it in one word – yes, we are comfortable. To us, it is our game plan. We know where everything is, where it came from, things that might even now be redundant have a cherished memory and we know what once they meant to us. For example, we don't use the electric grill as we once did to make toasted cheese sandwiches, but it still sits in the kitchen. Maybe we might fancy a toasty again one day, but it's part of our lives! Yes, it might look to the uninitiated to be a life of inconvenience and we would be better in a spanking new purpose-built flat or apartment, but we would have to leave all the lovely memories behind us. Do we want to start again? I think not. It would be too uncomfortable an experience.

One final thought on comfort. Teaching one day at a smaller hospital in the Group on cup final week. I was called to the office of the senior nursing officer and asked if I would talk to a surgical patient who had a malignant disease and after surgery was not doing as well as they thought he should. This man was an ex-serving senior engineering officer in the RAF, a Group Captain no less, and knowing my background I was asked to have a chat with him as nobody was really on his wavelength enough to talk with him. Most of the conversation in the ward among the other patients was about football and other sports and he appeared rather withdrawn from such trivia. He had been on the design team of the latest fighter plane in service at that time, so was a very clever and highly qualified engineer. He had left the country on discharge from the service and gone to live in South Africa, but became ill on coming home for a holiday. He had no relatives in this country. I went down to the ward and we got on like a house on fire. He laughed at my contribution to the RAF, saying I was only really, as he put it, 'Civvy attached!' But we exchanged stories about places to which we had been posted. The following week, I was telephoned by the ward sister. Would I go down? The patient was behaving strangely. I arrived at the ward to find the sister and staff nurse and a couple of student nurses standing outside the entrance to the bathroom, looking puzzled. "What's the problem?" I asked.

"It's the Group Captain; go in and have a look," they said. I went into the bathroom. There he was, lying on his back on the stone floor in his silk pyjamas, hands behind his head. The sun was streaming through the frosted glass windows, making it warm and cosy. He opened one eye and looked at me.

"You okay?" I asked him.

"I'm fine," he replied.

"Lunch in ten minutes," I said.

"Be there," he replied. I came out.

"What's he doing?" asked the staff nurse.

"Having a kip," I replied. "What's wrong with that?" She looked puzzled.

"I don't understand. Why on the floor?" I laughed.

"He's getting away from you all and getting a bit of peace from the football fans. And as for lying on the stone floor, if you'd ever lived in a hot country, you would have often done that." No, comfort is not just a physical thing.

CHAPTER 8

DIETARY NEEDS

Much time and effort can be spent deciding, planning and cooking meals either to order or just on the spur of the moment. Food is essential to life, of course, and regular meals are needed in the care of the sick and in particular when one's charge has a metabolic condition such as diabetes and the requirements of a soft, easily-dealt-with plateful when the patient is not all that adept at handling cutlery with diseases such as MS. Our meal planning has to take into consideration a lot of factors that are not even bothered with in normal health. Yes, it all adds up to make the days busy, and of course, it has to be cooked, eaten and the washing-up done, and so on. And added to this is the requirement for at least two litres of fluid a day to keep the bladder healthy and bug-free. The bladder when infected can be the cause of much distress to the immobile patient who can't get to the loo on time, but Sandie has a catheter and bag and this soon fills with the high fluid intake and needs a careful eye kept on it so it doesn't overfill and cause bypassing of the catheter, and the subsequent wet bed or clothing. Sandie likes a variety of flavoured drinks. Herbal teas are her preference. At the moment, we are on mint tea. Suddenly she decides to go on to another flavour – and who am I to deny her anything? And we end up with a lot of half-empty packets of tea bags which not only fill the space in the kitchen cupboard, but are expensive as they soon lose their flavour if you don't use them up in time when opened.

I am unable to go out shopping at present, so rely upon the online shop. Marvellous thing this, but it has its drawbacks like everything else in care; nothing is ever simple! Nothing really beats the trog up and down the aisles looking at all the goodies, and a lot of things you don't need, but they are all arranged on the shelves so that you don't miss anything and think *Oh, that looks nice. Wonder if she'd like some of that.* You don't get that online. It's rather clinical. You get what you see and that's what you do the shopping for, then when you close the page, you realise that that was not really what you wanted, was it? I have a standard shopping list, but still things get missed, or you press the wrong bit and get two of them by default! Also, you tend to get the same stuff week after week, and if you don't buy it, they remind you. With so much to do, it's hard to keep everything in mind.

Now, of course, with Sandie's new problem of diabetes, I spend a lot of time looking at the sugar content of the foods, and believe me, it's in everything, or almost in everything, so one has to be careful. It's the refined carbohydrates that are the problem with diabetics, and using specialist cookbooks for the diabetic would try the patience of a chef at the Ritz. I just do not have these wonderfully described substances in my kitchen cupboard which adds to the problem, things I have never heard of, but some people obviously have, but I manage without them. So among the thousand and one things in a day which keep us going is trying to vary our diet. It looks sparse, but I have to eat it too, so why am I putting on weight again and she is losing it? It has to be nutritionally acceptable, but looking back to wartime days, how my mother coped with such a limited range of foods I don't know. I still remember, however, the delicious smell of her steak and onion suet pudding (well, shin of beef – more likely to be available on the ration!), pervaded the house whilst cooking, and the taste when we got to it – "Absolutely magic."

Also, the admonition to we kids: "And eat your cabbage or you'll never grow up to be a big boy." I hated cabbage then; I still do, but it is one of the components of Sandie's diet.

I told Sandie about it the other day. She replied, "Nothing is as good as my mum's roast potatoes; yours are rubbish in comparison."

"Thanks for that!" I replied. I guess my end of term report will say, 'Must try harder!' However, she can't have too much suet pudding now, but I can never achieve the pinnacles of taste of those gastronomic delights that Mum offered us ungrateful kids!

And then we have the hunt – the-slipper practice of looking for those things that have 'no added sugar' and are sweetened with chemicals that bamboozle the taste buds but leave a nasty taste in the mouth. Even with normal diets, the health freak lobbies have got at the prepared food manufacturers and removed almost all sugar and salt to the detriment of taste. Certain prepared foods used to taste very nice, but now it's like eating blotting paper with all the flavour missing. Some commercial leek and potato soup (no sugar added, of course) I bought for Sandie from a very well-known food producer looked and tasted like washing-up water and was not a nice experience at all, and this is one of my favourite soups. Funnily enough, adding the absent flavouring agents before eating does not enhance the taste, so what else they have done with it, I don't know.

Drink is another problem. Must be sugar-free. Fortunately, Sandie does not like sweet or salty foods, but I do, and as a professional martyr complain volubly. This is when she throws her dinner at me, but we get by! There are a number of drinks now that are sugar-free for the diet fads but most of them, like fruit juices, are loaded with sugar, not only natural sugars but added refined carbohydrates to make them more palatable. The alternative is water, not a palatable choice. Out of the tap, the taste varies and goodness knows where commercial water comes from. It's like distilled water: utterly tasteless. But having an indwelling catheter, she must have a high fluid intake, so I do my best to vary her drinks as much as possible. But with hot drinks where some sweetness is needed, artificial sweeteners are not a good alternative to sugar, and cooking with them, I have discovered that their quality of sweetness reduces the longer you cook the meal. So it's all a bit of a learning curve until you get it right. And if by your actions or inactions, the diabetic patient ends up with urine full of sugar as the poor old kidneys try and get rid of it, the downside is that a bladder full of golden syrup is a good breeding ground for bacteria of the nastiest sort.

So it's a subject on its own that has to be mastered if you want to avoid trouble for your patient, and a lot of extra work for the carer if the patient becomes more sick than usual.

CHAPTER 9

WHAT IT MEANS TO BE A CARER

I am a very different person to the one I was ten years ago when I married Sandie. I've learnt an enormous amount, changed my attitudes to so many different things, got older! I have found myself working twenty-four hours a day, seven days a week, and 365 days a year with little rest and sometimes nights of broken sleep, not only caring for someone almost totally disabled and needing a lot of love just to survive, but trying to look after myself and a home with all its requirements – cooking, washing, shopping, etc. – but have still retained my sanity (just) and hope to continue for some years in the future. I have been asked how I manage to function day after day doing the same repeated tasks, all having to be done properly, sometimes as necessity demands, the same repetitive tasks done in a different way, but all correctly, or you have to go back and do them all over again. Sometimes as a result of a mistake, or lack of attention, if it is not remedied at once, you have even more work and Sandie is disappointed knowing how particular I am to get it right the first time. There is no putting off until tomorrow with physical care. The demands are immediate, painful pressure areas quickly become sores, constipation causes pain or subsequently incontinence, hunger causes a need for food, in

Sandie's case, sometimes urgently as she is a diabetic. Bladder discomfort means you must attend to it at once or infection can result, and so on. Sitting comfortably or lying correctly is essential or position can be a problem when, for example, feeding has to be done. Sandie, with only one functional arm, can never clear a plate of food and the carer can get quite a backache standing and feeding her if she is not in a good position. Neither carer nor Sandie are comfortable or the carer does it quickly to get it over with, and Sandie's confidence takes a plunge. These are only the immediate things. I find I need eyes in the back of my head sometimes to be aware when all is not well, and it's usually the little things that cause trouble to someone who is not in control of her space. Little irritations soon become big ones. In medicine, problems for the young often sort themselves out, but in caring for the older patient it becomes more difficult. I have met carers who think that to give another pill will sort out the problem, but it is usually easier to attend immediately to their wants before they change into needs which then do require more expert attention, and most carers are not either nursing or medically trained and have not learned to look for signs that all is not well, even though the patient may say, "No, I'm all right." I always recall the old psychiatric saying: 'Beware of the smile on the face of the depressive'. Listen to what the patient is not saying! Look, feel and understand; the clues are all there. Don't ignore them! It's almost like being a personal servant to Sandie, as she is unable to do most things. It is "Can you get this, pick up this, wash this, I'd like a cuppa, toilet, lay down, open the window, close it, sit me up a bit, etc. etc., never-ending. But if you don't do it, you don't care, so get on with it and enjoy the company of somebody you love, and by seeing that they are comfortable and have nothing to complain about, you too are comfortable with your life.

All this is difficult. Nobody said it was not, but if you are tired yourself, it is more difficult. The patient in pain may snap at you, and because you are tired, the unthinking word is said in response which may cause a lot of damage. You need a lot of patience and love to care for the sick, elderly or disabled and have to remember that you are fit and have no problems as the patient has, and learn to take it on the chin with a smile! You can't work with the sick if you feel unwell, or you will soon transfer your insecurity to them.

Yes, all this I had to learn, or refresh my memory when we got together again. But it is so worthwhile to see how she reacts when I do something for her that she likes and has been unable to do in all the years of her illness, often because nobody was switched on enough to realise that they were treating her, not her disease.

Yes, I listen to Sandie. Who listens to me? My GP asked me once, "Don't you have any help?"

I laughed. "Each set of carers I've had for Sandie I have had to supervise," I replied. "She, like most MS patients in their later years, has so many problems."

She replied, speaking directly to Sandie, saying, "Aren't you lucky to have him," and with that went on her way! Oh thanks, I thought. When I was first diagnosed with spinal stenososis and was unable to stand for long periods, I informed social services that I was to be admitted for surgery and would require help. They did a full assessment by the social worker and told me to inform them when my admission date for hospital would be. However, recalling Sandie's experience of their help before we got married, I decided on the advice of a friend who employed a private company to look after her dying relative, to contact this company. It was expensive at nearly 1K a week for live-in care but I had to bite the bullet. The operation came and went. I was discharged to rest and exercise for a few weeks, but the standard of care they gave was in my experience so inadequate that I had to supervise it constantly. Sandie's care as a totally disabled patient is complex, and on discovering that their training took only two weeks, I was most unhappy. These carers did what they thought was necessary and then just sat down, and one memorable day when one of them had nothing to do, she did just that, and sat looking at the garden for maybe an hour at a time in silence.

In my opinion, there seems to be a problem with both the social services and the private care companies. The social services are underfunded with too many patients to look after with the money available. The private companies appear to recruit staff of insufficient intellectual ability to perform well after a certain level of expertise has been reached, then if questioned about their slipshod behaviour, and I have complained to their employer that they have few nursing skills, they will give the same answer: "We are not a nursing agency." What, for heaven's sake, do they mean by that? Wiping bottoms carefully and cleaning teeth properly is nursing, surely. If they employed trained nurses, as I am, the job would be done properly because I know the consequences of bad practice! Whoever they are, if the task is done badly it's the patient who suffers! It was quite memorable that only one of the private carer staff did try and help me with the little things. She was a sweet, hard-working girl, and I told her employer I was pleased with her work, but the company took her away after a fortnight and replaced her with one who performed like a robot.

However, carers, good and bad, have to take it on the chin. It is not always a pleasant job, but the 'trainers' are not with the patient, and do not train them on patients, but the carers, after this training, are sent out, ill-prepared so far as I have seen, sometimes in twos indeed, to face the section of the public which is at its most vulnerable. In the case of the private carers, you have to pay and you get the time you pay for, and in the case the social services, it gives a job to the lower paid which suits the unemployment figures and so keeps the politicians happy! Social services depend on the money allocated to them and therefore are limited in what they can afford to offer, but the private services depend on the pockets of the patient, and they need to be very deep indeed as I have indicated. When are governments going to sort it out?

It takes a very special person to be a good, competent carer and requires that they have a flexible mindset. Each patient is an individual with his or her problems, often unique to themselves, and care cannot be practised in a one-size-fits-all method.

Sandie woke today at 7 am. By the time I had got her undressed, sorted out the bed, washed, dried and powdered her, half dressed her in her day clothes, unravelled her night urine bag and fitted her with her day bag, rolled her into her hoist, fetched the power chair after disconnecting it from the charger and brought it into the bedroom, hoisted her into it, completed her dressing of day clothes, adjusted her in the chair, adjusted the chair to her requirements, fitted her shoes and socks in position and secured her feet safely and strapped her in, took her to comb her hair, brought her into the dining room and settled her in her place whilst I cooked the breakfast, supervised her eating and given her morning medication, and so on and so on, one hour and five minutes had passed. Then I had to wash up the breakfast things, take her back to the bedroom, onto the hoist, onto the bed, take away the power chair and place it where I would not hurt myself, take off her trousers and underwear, hoist her onto the sanichair, into the toilet, insert a suppository, wait for it to work, wash and dry her, then back to hoist her onto the bed, get her onto the power chair and dress her again. We were ready by 10 am and ready for a cup of coffee. Then her hair needed washing, no quarter of an hour visit needed here. Privately, that would take two people and the cost of two hours each at £17 per person per hour soon mounts up. And this happens every day, not forgetting lunchtime, afternoon attention, and settling in bed at night, by people who, by and large, do not understand the concept of comfort! I do not think any of the many carers Sandie has had, that I have seen work, got it all right. There was always something very basic indeed that was not done well, all because "That's the way we were trained!" One carer memorably claimed there was too much furniture in the bedroom and stumbled over it: a bedside table and a commode, both on wheels; she didn't have the wit to move them out of her way! She ticked all the right boxes, however!

The patient is usually exhausted by all this, as is the carer! Can you avoid showing your feelings to the patient? You should not, of course, but those who go from one patient to another in the community, chopping and changing and knowing that others await their attention urgently, do they skimp the job? Probably, or they'd never get through the day, and then feel guilty about it all! They deserve sympathy if they are committed persons, as many are. What a job it is!

Yes, all this I learned when marrying Sandie. Did I volunteer for it without fully understanding just how much I would be doing? Up to now, others had done it for her, but now I know just what she so often complained of. They never had enough time to get everything done, or it was done in a way she did not approve of – no privacy, no compassion – but dared not complain, fearing that they would make her life misery if the carer was stressed and in a bad mood.

Most of the non-medical administrators of care have never done the job; bean counters are always concerned about money, but old and sick people deserve better than this. Yes, correct management is essential, but it is only the frame that proper care fits into.

CHAPTER 10

MEMORIES

S andie and I were discussing my background the other day, when I told her that one of the first patients with MS that I encountered in my training was a Mr Jackson in the terminal stages of the disease, aged some forty years. She was quite shocked to think that he had suffered for so short a time when she herself still had a reasonable lifestyle at her age of sixty-nine years.

"What was wrong with his treatment?" she asked... What indeed? Nothing really! There was none in 1947. He had septicaemia because of persistent pressure sores. Heavily infected as they were, there was no way these sores could be treated, only washed and dried with a bit of powder. There was little or no research that had been carried out on tissue viability in those days; antibiotics were only just coming into common use and were far too expensive to waste on bedsores! Physiotherapy was decried by most in the professions as 'slap and tickle!' There were few muscle relaxants or analgaesics that did not have serious side effects such as chronic constipation and confusion. Rubber urethral catheters which were sterilised by boiling, then used again until they wore out, were a conduit to bladder and kidney infection. Diet and supplements were little understood. In fact, his life was spent either immobile in bed or upright in a wheelchair, written off as incurable and usually confined to the local geriatric hospital for what was known as basic nursing care, and indeed, basic it was. Or he was cared for at home with the occasional visit from the district nurse. I cannot recall any great sympathy or understanding by any of my colleagues of just what the loss of control of the patient's life must have meant to him. We all thought it was sad, and hoped we never got that sort of disease, and I, along with my fellow students, was taught about disease and how to care for his physical problems, but we were not encouraged to talk to patients too much, because of the danger of 'emotional involvement' as it was called. It was considered a waste of valuable time, and that was that! As Sandie remarked, he was lucky to have survived so long, and yes, this was the outlook in 1947. There was no NHS, and medicine was advancing slowly, but it was going to take many years for the many systems and organisations to come to terms with the disease. The war, recently over, had given an impetus to the treatment of acute surgical problems such as trauma and burns, but chronic problems were confined to the back burner compared with all that is available to the affected patient today.

However, in the post-war era, we had more available care than in the time before the war. In those days, the chronic sufferer was confined to bed or to a sort of wicker carriage in which he was laid, and spent most of his time either by the fire – if the relatives could afford one (or even to buy coal) – until to the great relief and sorrow of his relatives he eventually died. In the Welsh valleys, many miners severely injured with broken backs or emphysema by their jobs had no recourse to help, and manufacturing industry had no

Health and Safety at Work Act to help relieve the burden on the stricken worker and his relatives, so looking at the social history of this land, one has to realise how far we have come, where today I can sit with Sandie, me at eighty-five and she at sixty-nine, with a lifetime of problems behind us and still enjoying the good things of life. How fortunate we are to be living in 2017 when many good people and organisations have the money and energy and inclination in particular to keep us going in a situation which is no longer just an existence, and in spite of it all, we are now living.

Thinking along these lines, Sandie reminded me that in her personal file she had found a letter written by her long-dead father in which he described his childhood and social conditions in South London prior to the First World War, and his life up to the time, when to avoid the law, he joined the regular army as a boy soldier. The letter was addressed to her grandfather. Why to him she did not know. Probably conscience, she thought, by which her father was trying to make amends for some misdemeanour, but whatever and why ever she had it in her file she could not recall. But when we extricated it from among old photos, it proved to be a historical document of possibly some value – certainly to researchers of the period – of the life of two naughty boys brought up in the privations of war with its subsequent hunger caused by the food shortages brought about by the German submarine warfare on British shipping, resulting in the family often reduced to eating black bread and pork dripping as their main diet for days at a time. He also describes the night the first Zeppelin was brought down by Lt Lief Robinson of the RFC in his Sopwith aeroplane, describing the ball of fire which ensued and the cheering of the onlookers on the ground, and the hero worship in the newspapers of the brave pilot thereafter. He also describes vividly in his letter the terrible retribution taken on their young bottoms by his irascible father when they were too naughty with a cavalry whip – a whip covered with canvas over a thin steel core – and being unable to sit down pain-free for a fortnight. One day, he and his older brother being left alone in the house, messing about as usual as children do, they knocked the overmantel mirror from the wall which promptly shattered into a thousand pieces. They were frantically trying to concoct a story to cover this disaster, fearing the whip again, when the whole neighbourhood was rocked by a terrific explosion which knocked everything else off the walls. The ammunition works on the Isle of Dogs had exploded, causing terrible loss of life and property, but they avoided the whip by reassuring their annoyed father that it was "the explosion what done it." Life must have been stressful as well as dangerous. The Zeppelins continued their bombing raids; they were also so hungry that as fourteen-year-olds, so far as we can tell, he and his brother irrationally left home to make their fortune elsewhere, but when he had his button up boots stolen when he took them off to rest his aching feet, he had to return home shoeless, where once again they were lashed with the whip. Shoes in their state of poverty were more than expensive to replace.

However, the social conditions of the poor working class of the time are well documented, but it is still worth noting that apart from 'Parish Relief', if there was no job there was no food. The next stop was the workhouse, the horrors of which are well described by writers such as Dickens, and little different even in those late times. But of course, war work gave money to the poor. Sadly, as this stopped after hostilities ceased, many families were at their wits' end as to how to fill the bellies of their children, and there were many of them, with contraceptives unavailable and health care only of a basic nature. It was either work, or steal, or starve, and finally the workhouse.

This letter, and the realisation of what they did not have, made us feel grateful for the many blessings we have today, particularly in health and sickness care. I do not cost the state a lot doing most of the caring myself, or paying for others to do it, but the facilities are there if we want them.

But to get back to the file. There was also, among the bits and pieces, a letter I'd written to Sandie prior to our marriage. It was to me now an embarrassing letter, written apologising for something – must have been nasty! – the subject of which neither of us could recall. I asked her if we should destroy it. She replied darkly, "No, keep it. I might find it useful one day!"

She laughed. "Oh," said I, "and the same to you with knobs on!" She laughed again. There was also a photograph of herself aged about six years old standing next to her father, he with a protective arm around her. He looked a nice, caring man. Of course, I'd never met him. "Must have that," I exclaimed and forthwith found a photo frame and mounted the picture in it, which now has pride of place on the dining room windowsill and we look at it fondly between mouthfuls!

Memories are wonderful things, the good ones that is, and to find documentary evidence is even better. It is so worthwhile keeping these little mementos to peruse when the skies darken, as surely they will and do.

CHAPTER 11

THEY HAVE EYES BUT SEE NOT, EARS THEY HAVE AND HEAR NOT, NEITHER DO THEY UNDERSTAND

Over the years there have been many people and professions involved in Sandie's care: medical, both conventional and unconventional, specialist nurses and consultants, social workers, social service workers and private care providers, and of course, two dear friends who are always available when needed, who spend their valuable time talking to her and taking her mind away from the mundanity of sickroom living, but more of them later. Most have an impact upon her for good or ill. It is difficult for many people to recognise the person in the wheelchair, and instead they see a victim of circumstances and are sometimes embarrassed by their good fortune in being well themselves, or reluctant to chat in any depth in case they say the 'wrong thing'. And indeed, many professionals see a case of MS in the chair and react accordingly, instead of seeing a person who has the disease.

But Sandie is in the unenviable situation of having an elderly husband who is limited in what he can do physically, in whom although the spirit is willing, the flesh is somewhat weaker, but writing as that elderly husband, my main task is to supervise what is done for or to her, and to give love and reassurance even on the darkest days. But more of that later, also!

I recall with amusement the visit I had to my GP, a most compassionate man, not long after we were married. He asked me after he had attended to my problem, "How are you coping with your wife, with difficulty?"

I replied, "Well, you try putting the socks on someone who has a positive Babinski's reflex."

He laughed, "Chasing her legs all over the bed, eh?" I must explain. When the normal reflexes are elicited with a patella hammer, as when the knee reflex is sought, there is usually a tightening of the muscles momentarily as the muscles concerned tighten and relax rapidly in a well-known way, but when the sole of the foot is ticked or tapped, the toes under normal circumstances tighten the foot into a ball, but with MS the toes bend upwards and outwards and the foot draws away, even if, as in Sandie's case, the legs are paralysed, making it difficult momentarily to put on socks when you inadvertently touch the sole of the foot.

This fact, to the uninitiated carer, is quite a surprise, having been told that Sandie is unable to move the leg, but it moves involuntarily if touched in a certain way. This, of course, demonstrates that the problem is not in the muscles but in the nerve supply to the muscle. One memorable morning, one social services-employed carer, on attempting to wash Sandie's feet, placed the bowl of soapy water on the bed itself next to her feet. She unwittingly touched the sole of Sandie's foot which automatically jerked upwards, spilling the water over the bed, necessitating an immediate sheet and blanket change. Placing the bowl to make the job easier by not stretching for the flannel, made her life a lot harder in the circumstances. She jumped back in surprise, saying, "Sandie, you didn't have to do that," totally misinterpreting the situation! No, the feet and legs look normal but certainly do not react as in good health. The other fact the carer discovers is how heavy a paralysed leg is because every time it requires repositioning and has to be moved, it can take some considerable effort and skill. Whoever said caring for the sick is easy? If that is what they think, they should try it!

Some of the most mundane tasks take a lot of skill. Placing a patient on a sanichair, for example, to take her to the toilet: get her just too far forward and she may fall off, too far backwards and toilet procedures following a bowel action are impossible, and then one has to take her back to bed without proper cleaning, and once again clean sheets are needed, unless the carer has remembered to put a paper towel on the bed, and the electricity bill goes up for the washing machine, and more time is spent unnecessarily which should be going on patient care. Sounds easy? Try it and see!

One morning, three days after surgery as I sat over breakfast, Sandie had had an urgent call to the toilet. Suddenly I heard her screaming. I heaved my aching body – I was one week post-operation after a spinal operation – jumped out of my chair and rushed into the toilet to find her falling off the sanichair, almost on the floor and the carer panicking in front of her, flapping her arms about and shouting, "What do I do? Oh, please help me."

I managed with great difficulty with my aching back to retrieve the situation and afterwards said to the carer, "When you are in that situation, just do something, even if it is only to pick your nose, but to stand helpless in front of a helpless patient magnifies the problem twice over and disaster follows swiftly, because the patient has now lost total confidence in you." This was so serious a situation because I had instructed her carefully in Sandie's care and checked that she understood, and I was so cross about it that I phoned her employers to complain, only to be told she had been tested on this subject of patient handling and had achieved a score of 80%. I suggested sarcastically that 100% would have been better, but exam marks did not prove her competent to care for sick or paralysed patients.

Their response was, "We are not a nursing agency; we are carers." That finally took my breath away and I lost patience and disposed of their services forthwith!

With a chronically sick person whom you love, it is very hard to see stupidity in their care, and is as painful to me as it is to Sandie. This is why, irrespective of the problems that arise, and every day there is something different, I like to assess them myself before requesting help from other sources if needed, and rarely do if I can avoid it.

Our two friends are both cases of *Cast your bread upon the waters and you will get it back many days hence.* Pat, Sandie's dearest friend, was new at the firm where Sandie worked before her illness. It was not a very friendly place, apparently, and Sandie took her under her wing and helped her through some of the procedures of the firm, for which she was so grateful, and ever since Sandie's illness has been a rock in a weary land to rest under whenever necessary, and I mean whenever: good at listening, washing and setting hair, sickroom cookery and so on. People such as Pat are saints and get little appreciation. She goes not only the extra mile, but as far as is needed, and doesn't complain, and there are very few like her. Emily is the other one: always available, a very present help, in trouble a good listener, and that to people like Sandie is vital. Emily has just retired from the education services with many a tale to tell. She, like Pat, has had her share of troubles which all helps when seeing Sandie, as she understands. Yes, there are others, but visiting the sick is not a first priority in the lives of many, but all callers are welcome even if their help is not needed at the time. But when they do come, and we are grateful to see them, and accept the offer of a cup of tea, why when they go do they not offer to wash up the cup? You also need training to visit the sick!

But there are things that Sandie likes to have done her way. She knows how she wants her hair to look, for example, but a quick brush by a carer whose attitude is "That'll do," would most certainly not do for the carer if somebody did that to her! Yes, it's the little things that matter, as indeed they do to all of us, but fit people do not think about things. They are on autopilot; when disabled, the simplest task becomes complicated, as I have remarked before in this piece. How do you put toothpaste on a toothbrush if you have only one arm?

CHAPTER 12

GETTING AROUND

S andie and I do not often go out of the house or garden. We have a converted van to take her power chair – the car is by courtesy of Motobility, good firm that! They really deliver on their promises. Nothing is too much trouble, and this is the third vehicle we've had from them to date and we have had some good trips out, and even holidays, because we have this facility. However, in my now somewhat debilitated state I find it difficult to strap Sandie and the wheelchair in together. It needs a bit of effort and my back knows it and objects strongly. I had to visit the chemist last week for some emergency medical supplies – nobody delivers on a Saturday! I enjoyed the short drive but felt very tired afterwards. Driving is all right, it's getting out and walking when you get there that is the problem! It only added a couple of miles to the milometer total, which now stands at less than 5k, which shows how little we use the vehicle, but it is good to have for emergency use and saves calling on friends once again for things I should be able to do, and indeed once could do with ease. But we did have a short ride in the country two weeks ago. Sandie enjoyed the drive but it took me forty-eight hours to recover my equilibrium!

No, it's a wonderful facility to have available, but the neighbours must wonder at times why such a nice vehicle spends so much time on our drive unused. So to make sure the battery does not go flat I asked our wonderful friend Pat if she would agree to go on the insurance and drive it shopping for us once a week to make sure it works. As it's shopping for us, we are not breaking any rules in letting her use it and it keeps it functioning properly. Indeed, Sandie is quite happy in the garden; she never really liked holidays, and although we have had some in the past, using the cars which were adapted for her condition, I think it is all the effort I have to make to arrange them and organise the exercise that is so tiring. You can take nothing for granted, and even though you book a cottage or something advertising disabled facilities, that's a catch all phrase and often falls short of what she needs, sometimes only little things, but it's the little things that matter. Sandie does find it difficult to cope with changing circumstances and really prefers stability and peace and quiet as she now tires so easily.

This present vehicle is one of many that we have had: both our own and those leased from Motobility. Before our marriage I owned a large Hyundai saloon which she liked, but it was difficult to lift her from her wheelchair into the front seat, so I found a local adaptation company who advised me to get a swivel seat. This replaced the front passenger seat, and by turning it round to face the door, it was now easy to lift Sandie in bottom first, turn the seat to face forward, then tuck her feet in, strap her in and off we go. It proved to be a most useful bit of kit and did the job well. This adaptation was only made by a North Yorkshire company, and we had to go to Accrington – of the football club fame – to get it tailor made for us, and got a parking ticket into the bargain, which annoyed me because the attendant declared that our blue badge was displayed upside down and he could not, or rather would not, accept it as genuine. We had to find somewhere to stay while the seat was fitted, so I checked out hotels on the Internet which had disabled facilities. There was only one, so I booked it for a couple of nights. It turned out to be a very posh country club with a fee commensurate with its name, function, and fittings! However, we had a couple of comfortable nights with very, very good food as compensation, and a pianist who played during dinner! All of this because, as I said, it was difficult to get Sandie off her wheelchair and into the car. On one memorable occasion, placing the wheelchair incorrectly, we slipped and ended up on the ground together, a tangle of arms and legs! However, having been in charge of a patient handling and lifting course, I could cope with that to Sandie's amazement. I think she expected to be laying there still until the ambulance arrived. I also purchased a mobile and portable hoist which could lift a patient off the floor. It came into its own one day when, larking about, I dropped her off her sanichair onto the bedroom floor, and again she was amazed at the efficiency of modern equipment. The hoist was as useful at home as when we had to go out to see the dentist or clinic and they required her in some other position to that of sitting for treatment, so we were well able to cope with a lot of life's worries now with more ease and less hard work, but it still isn't easy and requires a lot of practice, and learning from cock-ups!

However useful this method may have been, we needed some other way of taking the power chair she used at home with us for shopping, and our next three vehicles were fitted with a hoist so I could lift her out of the power chair into the front seat and then stow the chair in the boot. This meant I then did not have to push her around to add to the misery of shopping. She enjoys it, of course, but I'm a typical bloke: get in and get out as quickly as possible, and this was a lot easier.

Our latest vehicle is even better, a drive-in one for the chair, but having had a lot of surgery recently, add to that, anno domini, a potent mix, and I find even that method no picnic. But talking of picnics, when we did venture out a few weeks ago, when I felt a bit more capable of doing the business of securing and strapping both the chair and Sandie in, we went to our favourite place in the local forest to find that the parsimonious Forestry Commission had even slapped a £1.50 charge per hour for parking on the disabled car parking lot. They don't understand that it takes about thirty minutes to embark and disembark from the car. It's expensive enough when disabled, and thoughtlessness by the authorities adds that bit more. Incidentally, all the ten or so disabled plots were empty, so I assume it has put people off. But I had my revenge and picked about two pounds of delicious blackberries from their bushes! It's a wonder they didn't have a 'no picking' notice on those. That'll learn them! Oh, the trials of life!

CHAPTER 13

ELIMINATION
(POLITE TERM)

In the years up to our marriage, Sandie had been the unfortunate and often unwilling resident in many homes, hospitals and resorts of various and often dubious quality, and because of this was not only in a state of mental constipation, but also physically suffering from the real thing! Mental because those who were caring for her, as a rule, had not made the effort, or given time to try and understand the wants of a young woman of reasonable intelligence, having lost control of her life, now having to rely upon the goodwill of others, and sometimes that goodwill was totally absent. Physically, because somebody with MS and an automatic gut, who requires attention when her gut decides to work of its own volition, needs the sympathy of the carer to understand and not to complain even though it is part of the carer's task to deal with this problem, or she is left either in a mess, or in sheer discomfort for sometimes hours at a time or until 'we have a minute', causing her to feel, not like a paying patient, but a nuisance disturbing the even tenor of the day's work. And with an automatic gut combined with loss of any sensory indication, she requires constant checking and observation during the days that she is not incontinent.

I think as a race we are bad at bowels – embarrassed probably – as it is a subject rarely discussed until old age: not exactly a subject to deal with when you are having a pub lunch unless it is among a group of nurses or other professionals! But most nonprofessionally trained carers are tongue-tied and have difficulty discussing with a patient this necessary function of the body, which gives so much trouble when ill health arrives on the scene; they become shy or do not know the correct language, and resort to the basic childlike phrases such as:

"Have you been?"

"Did you go?"

"Any luck?"

A great friend of mine was a cleric; I recall when staying with his family one day at breakfast, the dear man looked at the box of Bran Flakes on the table and commented on the advertising tag on the side of the box which stated *Makes You Go*. He laughed. "There you are," he said, "makes you go to church as well!"

Yes, so often when asking a patient questions about his/her bowel action, they will say, "Have you been?" Been where, to the seaside? Or "Have you gone?" I assume the correct response in English to that is, "No, I'm still here!" These euphemisms must be a problem to those many carers today who do not have English as their mother tongue.

So many strategies have to be used to get the gut working, and as a professional I know them all and use them to keep Sandie comfortable, but fluid intake of an adequate amount, plenty of roughage in the diet, and in particular, time is needed to be successful in this aspect of health care; you can't rush it! When she announces that she is in need of a trip to the toilet, and on getting her onto the bed to take her clothes off, I quite often find that the act has already been performed. Well, what then? No good getting upset about it, but it does push up the water bill! But she needs to know that I don't mind.

The eventual reader of this may well ask why he is going on about this. It's not very nice, after all. True, but neither are sweaty armpits, or snotty noses, or MS, or incontinence, or halitosis, but as human beings we will all one day possibly suffer from one, if not all, of these things. Just wait; you'll get there, believe me! Just you wait. No, we rarely think about these things until they happen, and then just think how much it affects your life and how nice it is when you can find somebody who really understands to talk to about it all. And those somebodys, in a busy world which is constantly getting busier, are becoming hard to find! We don't think much about our health until something goes wrong, then when it hits us right between the eyes we wonder why, and sometimes the cause is our own fault but not always. But a lot of ill health could be avoided had we listened to our body when it protested.

When I was in practice I was asked to lecture students at my college on patient handling. I taught the students that when a patient came to you for a consultation, not only to listen to what they said, and what they did not say, but had you noticed say a tiredness or worry in their looks or demeanour, and statements – and funny some of them were – to try and make your mind up whether the patient was ill or just not coping with normal life. In illness there are often a number of obvious signs that all is not right, e.g. a rash or inability to stand properly from sitting, but it is the hidden things that gave the clue as often as not: simple things, for example, like a dry mouth causing them to lisp. Have a look in the mouth and there may well be thrush, and that may point to serious things like diabetes. Constipation can be present in all kinds of illness, and is sometimes present in good health, but it is always sensible to ask the patient about their personal habits. It is essential when dealing with patients like Sandie to be all eyes and ears, as often nice people don't always let their hair down quickly, or there are patients who tell you what they think is the problem, having looked it up on the Internet, added two and two together and made five! And probably frightened themselves to death in the process, hence the anxious look! I often look at Sandie and say, "What's the matter?"

She smiles and says, "Nothing." It's what she doesn't say that matters, and when I have found out what really is the matter and sorted it out, it can often stop a small problem escalating into something serious. She's not lying, just wants to save me the trouble. Oh, the problems in caring for your nearest and dearest! You shouldn't worry really and let your patient see it, but you have to at times when professional help is unavailable and you are on your own.

But the descriptions of illness are dependent upon the culture, age or profession of the patient among other things. I recall a patient of mine, having been to see her GP, complaining of "Something wrong with me chest, doctor, feels as if I'm full of water," and instead of being taken seriously was told, "Hope not or you'll drown." And when I examined her chest, and listened with my stethoscope, she did indeed have some fluid, but in the pleura, the covering tissue of the lung; it is called a pleural effusion. Yes, the woman wasn't very bright and a bit inarticulate, but that's how they come! When I studied Chinese medicine I was often amused at some of the descriptions of symptoms described by their system of medicine. 'The feeling of a little pig running around in the belly', for example, translates into English as 'butterflies in the stomach' or anxiety. Lot of pigs in China, but not many butterflies! Or my favourite, which well describes the hard non-productive dry cough of tracheitis: 'the feeling of a young fox clawing its way out of the chest'. Why a young one I don't know, unless it has not had time to wear out its claws! But this is culture getting in the way and can be a trap for the unwary, and the many different descriptions of trouble 'down below', well, the mind boggles! And men are as bad at describing these problems as are women. Many people describe their heavy cold symptoms as flu; wait until they get flu and then they'll know what a nasty disease that is! Also, those with a headache say they have a migraine. As a migraine sufferer myself, I would not wish that disease on anybody!

Sandie is also the unfortunate sufferer of leg spasms and spasms usually wreak their havoc at night as soon as the lights go out and her legs turn into quivering logs of wood. Not only distressing to her, poor darling, but it means a sleep-disturbed night for both of us until as the day dawns they begin to settle. Few drugs help for long. It would need a general anaesthetic to stop spasms when they are most severe. Sometimes spasms come out of the blue, sometimes when she is distressed or very tired, or the weather changes suddenly. A blustery east wind equates with Chinese thought as very unsettling, and blustery weather is often associated with liver conditions. The liver in Chinese thought is the great calmer-downer of the body, the organ that makes all systems work smoothly. We all know the expression when somebody is a bit tetchy: "You're a bit liverish today." The patient is in a state of agitation and bad-tempered, just like the east winds we get in East Anglia blowing off the sea. So to calm it all down I spend hours gently and calmly massaging both her feet, which I find helps a lot, and telling her I love her, which always does! I was not surprised when Sandie had a scan last year and was found to have two small liver cysts, but so have a lot of people, and they do no harm, so don't jump to conclusions in medicine! And after years of being fed so much useless medication, I'm surprised her liver works as well as it does! Leg spasm frequently occurs in the small hours. They are very distressing for her and prevent further sleep until they may ease as daylight returns. We have found new drugs which relieve spasm. And trying to get her trousers off to get her to the toilet when her legs go into severe spasm is a nightmare, as is putting them on again.

So, nobody made me do it. No, I volunteered, but I am aware that we are not alone. Many families and couples have to slog it out year after year to help and relieve their loved ones' feelings and symptoms; after all, the disease crept up on them. They never expected that one day they would be called on to do this, but where are you going to get anyone else to do it with love and compassion unless you do it yourself, or unless you are very lucky if you are unable to do it yourself? You can't buy love or compassion. So, you get on with it, and smile, and that really helps, believe me. And then you get ready for the next session, which inevitably comes and it's usually just as bad and difficult as was the previous one. But you can't quantify the reward you get when after a disastrous episode she settles down and goes to sleep in comfort with a smile on her face! Yes, it brings its own rewards!

But not only are bowels a problem; the waterworks, particularly as she has a catheter in situ, can be difficult, and a few times when she is restless, for some reason, the wound in which the catheter passes through her abdominal wall has bled. It invariably happens when she is asleep and we wake to a bed full of blood. It only takes the equivalent of a dessertspoonful of blood to make it look as if she has had a major haemorrhage. A little bit of blood goes a long way, believe me, and usually soaks through to the mattress for all the precautions you take. Blood is very mobile and concentrated stuff. A little goes a long way and stains clothing heavily if not washed straight away!

Chapter 14

"I feel hot"

As the seasons change and the air temperature fluctuates, there is always the problem of maintaining the core body temperature of the disabled patient. Able-bodied persons can adjust easily to changes in the ambient temperature, but the disabled are often unable to change their position, exercise, put on or remove clothing as necessary, use a fan, help themselves to warming or cooling drinks and so on.

Sandie always feels hot – she claims – and on the coldest day when I feel cold she says, "No, I'm boiling hot," and so she is, but suddenly it all changes, and she finds for some reason that she begins to shiver or asks me to put her wrap around her shoulders. Her inability to maintain her core temperature is most noticeable, if you know what to look for. The fit person's heat regulating centre efficiently adjusts to changes by making one move, shiver, feel ill or the thousand and one things that are beneath the level of consciousness such as heart rate change, or blood pressure variation, all help in the process of survival. The kidneys excrete more urine as the sweating decreases (and takes a lot of warmth out of the body this way). Such diseases, such as pituitary deficiency in diabetes insipidus, or mellitus, where the patient can pass litres of urine a day, leave the patient a miserable cold wreck of a person in winter, but fortunately this is not a common condition but one to be aware of if you are responsible for sick patients. So, fit people shiver to warm up, or drink plenty to cool down, and remove excess clothing. Clothing itself is changed as the seasons change: heavy, thick clothing for winter and thin, flimsy clothes for hot weather. But thick clothing does not necessarily warm you if it doesn't trap the air around the body. If you just wore nothing but a thick overcoat and nothing else in winter, you would be cold, so it's a question of pick and mix to get it right. Women wear layers of flimsy clothing and keep warm adequately, as several thin layers will trap a lot of air and so insulate the body from outside temperature changes. But all of this is something healthy persons do without thought; the disabled need help to do this. So it's a subject on its own!

We've had a very hot few weeks of summer which to Sandie have been purgatory, but now the autumn has arrived with only a few degrees drop in temperature. But the change to Sandie, although very welcome, comes as a surprise to her physiology, and I have had to change the duvet to a tog 10 from a very light cover she has been using, and I have had to heat her drinks from fifty seconds in the microwave to one minute to achieve comfort for her, so it's a question of trying to maintain the balance as she is unable to achieve it herself. And this inability to cope with change, of any sort, can be a problem when dealing with MS as it is with other elderly sick patients. In fact, in all aspects of care, watchfulness and understanding are more than essential. It is well documented that where elderly sick have to leave their accommodation for pastures new, the death rate climbs. We are indeed creatures of habit, and the older and sicker we become, the more the carer is beholden to be on his or her guard at times when change is even suggested. The thought processes of the immobile sick are different to those of fit people. Bad or even good news can be very unsettling; the change of carers to a different carer and the change of their bacteriologist footprint can spell trouble when meeting a different group of bacteria on a person. We all have a footprint of this sort, having got used to our own bugs. Being able to cope with somebody else's flora can spell trouble! Carers who, for example, look after their own youngsters, then come to look after somebody like Sandie and bring with them, on their clothes and hair, the bugs their kids have. Let's not forget how a child, when first going to school, usually meeting another lot of children for the first time, under the stress of the new life of school, gets all the infections the other kids have and brings them home to mum after meeting a new set of bugs. Even weather can upset the patient. I recall working in a unit for the chronic sick, which was fully air-conditioned, and like all such places, it had no opening windows. The temperature and humidity were totally controlled winter and summer alike, but the patients could see the outside gardens, and in winter with the snow, they felt cold, and in summer, felt hot. "It's all in the mind," the staff said. Maybe, but it was true.

So above all, the carer has to be aware of change and learn to manage it. To return to the subject of body core temperature, a drop of core temperature is a serious matter especially when it drops to the point where it can be called hypothermia, which can be a killer, particularly among the young or elderly sick, and in Sandie's case, the immobile patient unable to help themself. Most body functions in the cells are controlled by chemical action and need heat to make them work efficiently, but the brain is the most sensitive organ to heat change and sudden temperature drop is often first noted by the onset of confusion, as indeed is a sudden rise in core temperature.

The obvious answers in winter are a warm drink and movement and extra clothing and the opposite in summer. So to bang on about it, keep a close eye on your patient in hot or cold weather if they find it impossible or difficult to change their position! Many immobile patients feel cold even in hot weather, and when I see carers putting a rug or blanket over the knees of a sitting immobile patient, and forgetting to ascertain that the backs of the legs are also covered, then my temperature rises!

So each year we hope for proper winter or summer weather and sometimes get it, but to change the subject again somewhat, it's the hope that keeps us going! Without hope, where would we be? St Paul opined that faith is the essence of things hoped for. True, but not false hope; that is unrealistic. Sandie knows there is little chance after all these years that if a cure for the condition of MS was found it would repair all the damage done to her nervous system, but is aware that every now and again some treatment or method helps; all is not lost! She has never given up hope after all, what is the opposite? It's despair, and that is destructive. It's a good job we who were alive in 1939 did not give up hope that we would win the war, or we would have been like some countries who just lay down and let the Nazis walk all over them. Hope keeps us going!

A friend of mine went to a secular funeral the other day. Asking him how he got on, he replied, "Oh, it was wonderful." I was puzzled.

"How so?" I asked.

He said, "The presiding official and a friend of the deceased said the most wonderful things about him. The dead man sounded as though he was the most wonderful man who'd ever lived; I'm sorry I never met him." I pondered this statement a moment. But surely a funeral was not for the dead, but to give comfort to those left behind! *Yes*, I thought, *you say what a wonderful man the deceased was, but that doesn't help me. I've got to live without this superb figure.* The funeral surely is to give comfort to the bereaved, and whoever takes the funeral is there to show them how to cope now that this paragon of virtue is no longer with them to guide their faltering footsteps with their example. In a Christian funeral, it is about hope: hope that one day, if we believe it, we will meet again in another world. No, you cannot prove that will happen, but neither can you prove it won't, and that is the comfort that hope gives you. As I said before, the opposite of hope is despair. Nobody told my friend how to cope without George. Maybe the alcohol at the party after the funeral would help ease the sense of loss he felt at George's demise.

CHAPTER 15

MOVING AND LIFTING SKILLS

Over the years, patient handling and lifting has altered beyond all recognition. In my young days, different methods were used as taught by different medical and nursing schools. There was no standard approach to the subject and, indeed, I do not think a lot of thought or concern had been given to it. It became almost a rite of passage to be admitted for back pain among the nursing staff, but then some enlightened soul decided it was becoming almost epidemic and needed looking at with an intelligent and physiological approach to try and stop the careers of injured nurses being destroyed because 'that's the way it's always been done'. So it slowly became recognised as a problem to be solved. With the advent of the NHS, many more elderly and chronically sick patients were now being treated, and with this came an increase of sickness among the staff with 'bad backs' and among the patients with dislocated shoulders, and so it slowly became a nationally recognised problem in hospitals, and with the difficulty of finding enough nurses and retaining them, an answer was desperately needed.

After a lot of research, the 'lifting courses' were instituted with well-educated trainers, often physiotherapists, who were expert in the science of movement of the body and who became an essential part of training, and very good some of them were, teaching safe handling for both nurse and patient. Some ideas, such as one of the first, imported from the Antipodes and called obviously the Australian lift, was the first most successful as a method of moving a heavy patient up the bed postoperatively. It needed two well-trained nurses to do it, but one of the problems we found in nurse education from the ward staff was, "What do those teaching lot know about it?" But we persevered and various methods slowly came into common use. But then, of course, came the Health And Safety at Work Act, and very good legislation it was too, but it was hijacked by the lazy and work-shy and could be used for whatever situation was unfamiliar to the operative not to do something because "The act says." They didn't know, of course, what the act did say but slowly it gained ground until all nursing staff were forbidden to lift, and with that came the increase in the number and severity of pressure sores among patients but fewer bad backs for nursing staff because we now had hoists.

Since time immemorial, all bed patients, before they went to sleep and woke up in the morning, had been treated to pressure area care which consists of washing the patient's bottom with warm, soapy water, and applying some methylated spirit, then drying with a dusting of talcum powder. It did work to a certain extent and hardened the skin, but as we pulled the patient up the bed after this, the layers of soft skin underneath could shear and you had a bigger sore. Then came the ritual anointing of whatever was the favourite ointment or potion of the time, and sometimes it did heal, but not always. I can recall seeing patients with such severe sores eroding the tissues down to the bone with such an infection that they did not survive. I have seen such things as Marmite and some types of honey used as a dressing: all good ideas, but they didn't always work; that was the trouble!

So nurses had to work very hard just to keep their patients reasonably well without the benefit of anybody thinking it through, using methods Florence Nightingale used all those years ago! Yes, the nursing profession were a conservative lot, believe me.

It was in the 1960s or later, when I was working on an orthopaedic ward, that we had a very large patient who had fractured his femur through ingesting loads of steroids which he obtained from somewhere, illegally probably, and was taking a large dose a day because "They make me feel good," he claimed. The result of this frolic was osteoporosis and the subsequent erosion of his femur head. He was, of course, totally bedbound with that condition in those days. He was also dirty and unkempt, and before what was then major surgery – no hip replacements in those days! – bathing in the big bath was ordered and it took six of us to get him in it and out of it. I'm not sure who was the most exhausted: the patient or ourselves. One day, a rep appeared at the office door with a large machine called a 'hoist' for lifting patients. We had never seen one of these before, but as he demonstrated it to us with its function of lifting even the most disabled patient, I realised this would do the job of getting our large, scruffy patient into the bath using only two nurses, with no danger to either the staff or himself. It proved to be successful and the rep allowed us to keep it for a week, and we used it for so many patients that it became an essential piece of equipment on the ward. However, one day, an 'authority' visiting the ward asked what it was. I told him what it was for and he replied, "Get it out of here, unauthorised equipment. Anything going wrong and the patient will sue." So it went, and the next day my colleague hurt his back lifting the scruffy patient, and he was put to bed on traction for a month.

At the end of the month, as I went to accounts to collect our pay slips, I gave my colleague his and he said, "Look at the tax I'm paying." I looked at the slip and saw his salary for the month was exactly the cost of one of the hoists. "Give that to me," I said and took it to the 'authority'.

He looked at it and said, "Point taken; okay, you can have one," and so every ward was eventually issued with one! Yes, anything new was looked at with suspicion in the nursing profession. We have moved on from there, but not a lot! We still have many entrenched attitudes.

But the use of all equipment has to be well taught or its use is fraught with difficulties, and harm can come to the patient through carelessness. I think one of the most important things when using this equipment, believe it or not, is silence. If the operators chat among themselves about other matters, they may fail to notice maybe just a little thing, but it's then it all goes pear-shaped! At times, we have had private carers to look after Sandie when I was in a post-operative state, and although they have been told how to use them, they have only practised on each other, and as I have pointed out before, hoists are not for fit young women having a good time, but for patients who have little or no control of their situation either physically or mentally. They are not toys for the uneducated and unthinking! It is quite amazing how much trouble carers get into when using them. I recall one morning after Sandie had been admitted to hospital, I was woken up at 8 am by the staff nurse on her ward – would you believe it! – saying that Sandie wanted to use the toilet: "How do we get her on the sanichair?"

"Have you ever heard of a hoist?" I enquired sarcastically. She said she had; they had one somewhere. They did find it, and when Sandie came home she told me that they made a mess of it and hurt her, so she did not have the bowel action, being too frightened to perform, and returned home with a very loaded and uncomfortable bowel and dirty drawers.

If the sling is not placed properly under the immobile patient, then the patient, when finally positioned in her chair, is uncomfortable and remains so until her position is changed and you have to do it, so more unnecessary work. It is difficult at times to keep one's mind on the job, especially if either the patient or the carer has something to say, or if there are two carers who choose to chat with each other, discussing things that do not concern their charge. When you are in charge of somebody's care you have to try and think as they do, and even think for them if they are at all confused or able to do little for themselves. This goes without saying, but does require a particular skill and is one of the many prices you pay in your chosen activity: to learn to put yourself a good second! It's your patient's welfare that you are there for, and if it is not your relative, it's what you are paid for.

No, hoists are not toys; they are, when used properly, valuable tools in patient care. They cost a lot of money so should be used carefully, thoughtfully and at the appropriate time, and used by trained operators whose mind is on the job in hand.

CHAPTER 16

LONELINESS IN SICKNESS

F eeling alone and deserted by the NHS one day, then help arrived like a 78 bus and three more behind! Three specialist nurses, a district nurse, two phone calls from our GP and a couple of friends, all concerned for Sandie's health, and a letter requesting information about our situation from the council. It is very comforting when this happens; little and often would be preferable and does not really make up for the apparent absence of attention. Yes, I know; all very busy people, as am I. We are living in a busy world, and I often need a twenty-five-hour day! And often even that would not be enough.

Our MS nurse visited us first. We had notice by an official letter that she was coming; this was a pleasant surprise. She had been sent to us by our new GP, a new one in the practice who took over Sandie's case about a month ago and got the ball rolling. This visit was followed by the diabetic ophthalmic consultant, then the diabetic nurse specialist, then the district nurse to take blood specimens, then the chemist brought a leaflet offering us a free flu jab, and last but by no means least, a dear friend who, when requested by Sandie to get her some fruit if she had the time, did just that and we were now the owners of a cornucopia of peaches, bananas, and nectarines. The kitchen was awash with it all. Good for the bowels! Hope the drains can cope!

But it was our new GP who got the logjam cleared: a youngish chap who came and was prepared to listen intelligently to our problems, and is prepared to talk to me using the same language as a fellow practitioner, even though we operate at a different level. He started it all following Sandie's discharge from hospital where she languished for nine days, unaware of what was happening, suffering from the result of a PUO (pyrexia of unknown origin) and telephoned to enquire after her progress to date. This was a surprise; when I was discharged from hospital twice in the last year following two bouts of major orthopaedic surgery, nobody bothered even to see me until I made a fuss!

Occasionally, I am asked – but not often – "How is Sandie?" on those rare times when I am able to get out and meet people. I don't know if this is just politeness or a genuine concern for her as she rarely goes out of the house or garden – mainly from choice, I hasten to add. The enquirer then usually responds with platitudes. I see little point in giving them detailed information or the response is often preceded by the statement, "Well, I'd have thought…" or "Why don't you try…" etc., etc. or "Keep taking the tablets": statements which purport to show concern, but I do wonder sometimes from what deep well of knowledge and understanding of medicine these remarks are drawn. These usually useless remarks come from that lexicon of well-worn stupid statements entitled 'Well, you've got to say something, haven't you!' And don't help in the least, just demonstrating that the enquirer is either embarrassed, or just plain unaware of what day it is!

The diabetic specialist nurse sent to us by our GP was of the same calibre as he: understanding and willing to listen to the feelings and emotions of a patient who has little control of her world and needs to delegate all decisions to others she can trust. And so this person proved to be, and the outcome of her intervention was first-class, with Sandie for the first time in months showing signs of being able to cope better than heretofore. Added to this, she was chatty; it was nice to catch up with all the hospital news that I knew so well all those years ago. Again, here was somebody who spoke my language and could appreciate the difficult situation I was in with so much knowledge. Where loved ones are concerned, you are sure to look at anything new and almost expect the worst! And this time it didn't happen!

Also, the MS nurse from firsthand knowledge was able to assure Sandie that she knew only too well the way that those patients who have lost control of their lives due to illness can be treated, but maybe not deliberately badly, by their carers. She discovered this when for some years she cared for a very close relative who then passed away. She is also a valuable source of information about developments in diagnosis and treatment, and care of those needing her services, but also the possessor of a pleasing personality which is a nice suprise for Sandie when she visits.

So no, we are not completely abandoned – even though it feels like it at times – and being well versed in all aspects of care, I do need reassurance at times when the candle burns dim, usually in the middle of the night when a bedroom feels almost like a prison containing two prisoners! But we admit that these professionals are busy people, and there are many in our situation, and I'm sure some manage to cope, some better and some less well, as we do. But the source of comfort we would prefer is what should be the role of our relatives and friends who rarely remember us apart from cards at Christmas and birthdays, assuming that no news is good news, and as we do not complain but get on with life the best we can, rarely, if ever, do we see any of them. Considering the huge number of persons I have seen and treated over the years, I assume they have not all died!

One of our favourite visitors is our vicar. He is a clever man, being a physicist before he took holy orders, and also taught sciences, so is aware very much of how the world works, both physically and spiritually. He is good company, but it surprises me that rarely do we see anybody from the congregation but himself and one faithful friend, who has enough troubles of her own, but finds time for us.

One of our greatest bugbears is the non-appearance of those who promise to come or phone at a certain time and do not. Life as we lead it is very proscribed in that those things that fit people do without a thought can take up an immense amount of time, and all has to be fitted into a day when Sandie is up in her chair. It can take a minimum of half an hour to take her to the toilet, get her on the bed first to remove clothing, hoist her onto the sanichair, into the bathroom, then wash and clean her up, then back to the bedroom and onto the hoist, back onto the bed, redress her, back onto the hoist and get her into her power chair without forgetting her glasses, her call alarm, her handkerchief etc., then back out into the room again. So it goes on, and this can happen four times a day along with all the other things she needs. If the visitor does not come, or is late, everything is thrown out of kilter by just waiting around and being unable to start the next task until they have gone, and that can extend the working day immensely.

So this is our life; if a visitor says they are coming, my message is, "We love to see anyone who is interested in us, but come when you say you will or please let us know if you will be late, or not coming. Yes, our life is complicated. The normal things of life take up to four times as long, but we get by, but have to fit a lot in. A simple task can take four times as long as when it's done by fit and healthy people. And please, do offer to wash your cup after a cup of tea if the patient is unable to do it competently themselves and I am too busy!"

But surely Sandie is not lonely. "She has you with her all day and night." I've heard this remark before. Yes, try and live in prison; you'll be lonely, unaware of the good things in life, and unable to get at them. She, like so many other paralysed people, is in the prison of a body that is going nowhere. I recall one day at the school of nursing being disturbed by a lot of laughing and chatter in the corridor outside my office, which was disturbing the conversation I was having with a distressed student. Going out into the corridor, I found a whole class of other students, half of them leading a fellow student with scarves around their heads and having a jolly good time. "What are you doing?" I asked their tutor who was supervising this class.

"Showing them what it's like to be blind," she replied.

I laughed, "No, you're not; you're showing them what it's like to get around with a scarf around their heads. Blindness usually, unless caused by some specific curable condition, is forever. You can't give these students the idea that they will never see again when blind, and the damage that does to their very life by doing this." No, surely in the waking moments of the blind, the thought of *Oh dear, another day to get through!* can be experienced, and using such trite sayings as "Oh, you'll feel better tomorrow," by the carer, should be replaced with "What can I do to help you get through today?"

Yes, chronic illness can be a lonely world, but can be partially filled if shared with a sympathetic carer or companion. Loneliness is a thing we all experience, indeed, but can be experienced in even crowded surroundings. I recall for some years commuting to London by train; nobody spoke to you if on your own, and then the truly British and unique experience on the underground: carriages full of silent passengers where it was almost a crime to talk! And all this in the biggest and most affluent city in the world. The loneliest place on earth! I have known the elderly in retirement homes, surrounded by other residents, to say their rest home was a lonely place. Yes, of course, if you are not listened to or ignored.

CHAPTER 17

MEDICATION AND NURSING TECHNIQUES

Many times I have been, if not exactly confused, somewhat bemused at the scope of the multiple prescriptions Sandie has had over the years. It's all in her records and makes depressing reading as few, if any, of these drugs and medicaments made any difference to her progress, and some I'm sure have sent it temporarily into reverse with their side effects. They have been either wrongly prescribed, or overprescribed, or have been used to see what would happen when she took them.

When Sandie first came to see me in my practice, she was on a virtual raft of drugs, antispasmodics, and analgaesics like Co-codamol – she was only persuaded to stop these two months ago; she must have kept the shares of the company afloat through hard times! Extra special vitamin preparations – good money-spinner, those – cod liver oil – somebody said it was 'Good for MS' – if only they'd treated her instead of MS, we might have got somewhere! Cannabis preparations – at that time the in-drug for the condition. Oil of evening primrose – good for women's health – at least they were thinking of her for a change! And so I could go on, with antibiotics for minor infections and Prozac – but she wasn't depressed – the list over twenty-eight years is almost endless, and none arrested the disease. Yes, they tried, but the only treatment to have any effect to help her condition was when a nasty bout of trigeminal neuritis – a fairly common condition to those with MS – hit her out of the blue. It was surgical intervention that gave her comfort from this distressing condition.

So I married a virtual pharmacy as well as Sandie! And a lot of her time was concerned with useless drugs, potion applications, and so on, but it's hard to persuade someone that the stuff they are on is useless, as it often is, when it has been part of their life for so long. By removing the familiar you are now venturing onto foreign territory. So I cut down, with the agreement of her GP, many of these useless things and she is no worse without them. I have to lay the reassurance on heavily anyway, but she might as well take something that works, rather than a prescription that sends the GP away feeling that he has done something!

So where are we now? With an automatic bowel, drugs don't help; it works when it wants to, and if it does not, laxatives take at least twenty-four to thirty-six hours to work. Then we have the washing machine functioning full-time, so bowel washouts and simple enemata help better. Time-consuming maybe, but not as time-consuming as forever changing and washing sheets and towels. The bladder problems of the paraplegic are well known, but it is my proud boast that only once in ten years has she had a blocked catheter or a bladder infection. Weekly washouts of the bladder with citric acid keep the bladder free from crystals of urea and so on, and again prevent wet clothes and sheets that can happen – to the distress of Sandie who hates that – as do changes of the catheter every one to two months (as a qualified nurse I am permitted to do this) and weekly changes of urine drainage bags. Pressure areas require constant attention by changes in position and utter cleanliness of the tail end. Washing with soap and water after bowel actions is vital. Numerous times I have had to tell carers when they were attending her and I could not, that they were not to use toilet paper, but to wash each time, again time-consuming but not as much as having to see to the unpleasantness to both carer and Sandie herself of a pressure sore or lesion to the perianal region due to rough handling. Fingernails and toenails need a lot of love to get them right. Each time we have had a chiropodist see to them, they have infected her nail bed in at least one toe, so I do them myself and am most particular that I use sterile equipment each time. The danger of this to the diabetic is well know and many a case of gangrene has been aggravated by dirty procedures. And so there is little I don't do for my dearest wife, and love doing it, and she knows it and trusts me!

But every now and again we get into uncharted country, as when she was admitted with a severe pyrexia (fever) of unknown origin and needed hospital admission. I have commented on this before, but by the time the infection was sorted out, with her diabetic state, as often happens, her leg spasms increased to the point where they were in spasm for nearly all her waking hours. When she came home, the drug Baclofen, a useful muscle relaxant, failed to work and she was now night after night in agony with her legs twisting all round the bed, with me chasing them! I was able to help with constant massage, stretching of her legs and other tricks to keep some sort of normality, but it was wearing for both of us. Believe me, the light at the end of the tunnel burned very dim as night after night I was up dealing with the poor darling, until she went to sleep and woke in the morning exhausted. But thanks to a combination of the MS nurse, the physio and the GP, who prescribed an analeptic drug that suited her, we now had comparative peace and she once again had some good nights' sleep. But after a few weeks, unfortunately, we were back to square one again.

But of course when Sandie was first diagnosed in 1984, there was little, if anything, available to arrest the disease. Today there are many things that help; but it's too late for Sandie. The damage is done, and a lot of the unsympathetic treatment and so-called care she has received over the years have certainly not helped. These last ten years, although we have had our ups and downs, she is possibly more physically stable now than she was when we first married ten years ago, and I put that down to love and the circumstances we have in our quiet but contented life. Treatment, however, is one thing, only one part of the equation. It's care and love that make it work – and trust.

However, the spasms went on, apparently untreatable and often for the poor girl, unbearable. Her legs in total spasticity – or clonus to give it its proper name – or flaccid and useless, but often painful after a bout of the spasm, and often to be more than worrying as soon as she went to bed at night, usually starting with bizarre movements in either or both feet and legs as she laid down, and all I could do was to gently massage them sometimes for half an hour before they relaxed and she got to sleep, until an hour later her legs flexed and outwardly rotated to her distress and discomfort and she was awake again. In my experience, the use of muscle-relaxing drugs is useless, but our GP tried to use an analeptic drug and for a time this helped to reduce the severity of the attacks and she did, with massage, and movement of the legs to get the blood moving, get some rest and some disturbed sleep. When the legs did relax, putting them through the full range of movements did at times help, but the residual pain was always there. Ordinary pain-relieving medication did nothing; it would need a general anaesthetic to completely calm down clonus.

But to my surprise, I found a few weeks ago that when the clonus does stop, and even when the pain persists, that gently palpating the muscles particularly in her left thigh, her abductor muscles were very sensitive to deep pressure, but by placing both legs in line with her body, and getting them to rest with both feet pointing in the position of function, the pain eased. So tying a scarf around both thighs, bringing them both together by wrapping the scarf around both knees and securing it with pins, the pain was almost dissipated, and she had the best night's sleep for weeks. We now secure her legs at night like this, and instead of her legs wandering around the bed all night in her half-sleep, she wakes in the morning having slept really well for the first time in years with the legs remaining in the same position in the morning when she wakes. This method also helps when during the day she is in her power chair. I also elevate her legs at night to encourage her circulation and encourage venous drainage and these methods are now a standard way of dealing with the problem. For the first time in years she now gets quality sleep, which for both of us is so much better than the years I have spent at night trying unsuccessfully to get her total relief. There is also, of course, with this regime, a general improvement in her well-being, and for the time – I hope for always – a much more comfortable life for her, which she does deserve.

CHAPTER 18

THE SKIN...
AND ITS PROBLEMS

Until three years ago, Sandie was free from the perils of pressure sores. When first we met, she had a callus on the outer side of her left foot, caused by the inattention of whoever her carers were in those days, allowing her feet to rub together in bed at night during painful spasms of both legs. This callus has now gone, thanks to constant repositioning of her limbs at night, but could soon return if this problem is ignored again.

But three years ago, following a period of intractable constipation which defied all conventional treatments, she was referred to a gastroenterologist who, being unable to find the cause of the problem, ordered an MRI scan which showed nothing of note, but he suggested the use of golden linseed as a remedy, and it worked well. However, she had been admitted overnight for a bowel preparation prior to the MRI, and with her automatic bowel, the contrast medium was ejected into the bed unbeknown to her, being unable to move her pelvis or sense the problem. She was allowed to lie in it until morning with the result that when she came home I found she had a large chemical burn on her bottom from the medium which has troubled her at times since.

The burn, of course, immediately became infected. I sent for her GP who prescribed the standard antibiotic and steroid creams and dry dressings, but to no avail, and she was seen by the district nurses and other doctors at the surgery, and was eventually referred to the dermatologist. Neither did his treatment work, although it was more effective than the others, and so it has gone on… frequent dressing changes, careful hygiene after each bowel action with soap and water, no toilet paper(!), frequent position changes and the addition of special pressure-relieving cushions and an airbed. Until some six months ago, being worn out with all the work which by now I was doing as I managed to keep it from worsening, I'd had enough. One morning, as I sat in the only place I can get any peace – the toilet! – I shut my eyes and as I sat there, I prayed, "Oh Lord, what do I do to heal my darling's sore bottom?"

A second later, a well-spoken voice said to me two words: "Salt water." Yes, I actually heard those words! It took me back to when I worked in a burns unit many years ago and we used saline baths and saline dressings, and they worked! So began a four-times-a-day salt and water wound wash and wet saline dressings, and within two weeks it had healed. Don't let anyone say God does not answer prayer! However, by the nature of things, the healing scarred but has been unstable since and requires constant observation and immediate attention if it shows signs of breaking down. A pressure sore on that part of the anatomy is always a problem, and when the patient is immobile day and night, even more so. So I just keep plugging away, hoping for the best and find that Johnson's Baby Lotion keeps the skin in reasonable condition. At least she does not now need dressings and there is no pain. Even the district nurses were impressed by my actions; I hope they learned something from this episode.

Another problem is toenails, and trying to trim nails as one chases the feet all round the bed is a nightmare, but when we had a chiropodist try, he trimmed the nails but infected a nail bed, and she needed antibiotics, so I do it myself now carefully with very clean instruments. There is no easy way; you just wait until the spasm passes and then be ready to leap at her feet, do it, and stand back as the spasm returns almost as soon as you touch her feet. Hard work? Well, it's got to be done, so you brace yourself and get on with it, hoping each time it will be easier than the last time! Then put the strap back on, tying her thighs together which controls the spasms.

But it's general health that makes sure she stays as fit as possible. But now as a diabetic, the old regime of a normal diet containing lots of naughty things such as refined carbohydrates is no longer possible, and I have to use a diabetic cookbook or just do my best and make the menu up myself with as many fresh and suitable ingredients as I can find. Funny thing is, she has lost weight; but eating the same rubbish, I still put it on! So long as her skin remains intact she does well, but any lesion, with her condition, has to be attended to at once. Keeping her skin warm, dry and clean, insofar as it is possible, is essential for health. The skin, after all, is the barrier to the living world and as the old advertising phrase for wrapped sweets has it: 'It keeps all the flavour in and the dirt out'.

But above all, the maintenance of comfort, both physical and psychological, needs attention at all times. For someone who has lost so much, she needs constant reminders that she is loved and needed; in fact, I need her as much as she needs me. There is little she can do to make a physical contribution to her world, so I have to think for her and do what I know she needs and wants to make her life just that, or it becomes no more than an existence, giving somebody else a job and little more than that. I recall some years ago when we were referred to a neurologist, he listened carefully to what we both had to say, and when I told him I did not need others to physically care for her because I loved doing it myself, he commented, "An example of total symbiosis." Yes, that's the trick; we work as one. Anything that worries Sandie, worries me, and anything that pleases her, is also my pleasure.

CHAPTER 19

HYGIENE

Most women are fastidious about the state of their cleanliness, and Sandie as a disabled person is no different, but in her case this desired status so often depends upon the understanding and/or goodwill of those who care for her and if they are prepared to listen to what she wants and likes. However, in her case if *Cleanliness is next to Godliness,* she may well be a resident – or have a place booked – in what John Bunyan referred to as the Celestial City! And, of course, a large amount of my time is spent ascertaining that her needs meet her own required and desired high standards of hygiene.

But there is one aspect to this concept if it is to be achieved as required, and that is that one cannot hurry these tasks. If you do, you have to go back and do it again, and this doubles the time needed to do the job, so there is, therefore, no saving in the end. Not only that, but a skimped or hurried task shows the patient that you have only limited time for him, instead of having him as the main person in your thoughts at that time. Again, if you do not have your mind on the job and prefer to discuss with a colleague those things you did last night, the effect is the same and the patient loses confidence in you as a carer.

So there are many 'bits' of a patient to think about, each requiring a different technique. It goes without saying that you can't wash somebody's bottom using the same flannel or materials with which you wash their face, nor can you clean toenails with a toothbrush. When you wash yourself you have your own methods of body wash, feet and toes, hair, teeth, ears and so on, so it is essential that you know from the patient his/her preferences before you start, and of course in these days where ethnic minorities may be under your care, don't forget the cultural taboos which also exist and which you may ignore at your peril, to the patient's discomfort.

But in Sandie's care, the most important aspect is care of her catheter and absolute cleanliness when having anything to do with her toilet and elimination. The catheter also needs washing through weekly, repositioning as necessary, all bags and holding straps cared for properly so there is no danger of them kinking or coming apart with the subsequent wet bed and clothes. The incision in the abdominal wall through which the catheter is implanted into the bladder must be kept scrupulously clean at all times or a painful sore may develop, which with the rubbing of the catheter when she moves makes it very difficult to heal and is very uncomfortable. A diabetic patient is more likely than others to get a urinary tract infection and this must always be first in your thoughts, and a careful eye must be kept on the urine in the bag and it be noted if there is any cloudiness or excess debris, change in colour, also if there is an unpleasant smell, all of which can be pointers to the fact that there may be infection present. So it needs close attention at all times.

Every six weeks, the indwelling catheter needs to be changed and a new one inserted. I choose to do this myself, being qualified, and it saves calling in the district nurse each time, who has enough to do. This is, of course, an aseptic procedure, and not only is strict asepsis needed but a lot of care shown, indeed the carer needs to be very careful not to cause trauma by handling the equipment as gently and kindly as possible, not only in putting the new catheter in, but in removing the old one which may have an accumulation of debris round its tip. One must never forget that a catheter is a foreign body, and the body does not take kindly to being invaded by plastic tubes, and as a protective deposit of white cells form around it to protect the delicate lining of the bladder wall, small amounts of cells can accumulate on the catheter, making it less smooth if it is not changed frequently enough. There is little one can do to ease the pain of removal, apart from ensuring that Sandie lies as flat as possible. To insert the tube: a gel containing a strong local anaesthetic eases the way in considerably when injected into the incision. If it is not done almost straight away, the incision closes slightly and one needs to push firmly to get the catheter in, even with the local. It is essential that the whole action is therefore done quickly and I prefer to do it myself because I am so used to doing this, and sometimes other professionals mess around a bit, which not only causes pain but makes Sandie apprehensive, and that makes what can be a not exactly pleasant experience for her, a thing to dread. Often there is some bleeding caused by this, but that is usually where the skin, in trying to close this artificial hole held open by a tube, responds by overgrowing a few cells – called granulation tissue – which is very friable, and therefore likely to bleed even if touched, but soon stops – fortunately. So I do it as quickly as I can and ensure, as far as possible, that I do it myself. Her standard leg bags are changed weekly. These give little or no trouble; these drain into a larger bag at night which is emptied each morning. This has a drainage tap which has occasionally been forgotten and left open – not by me, I should add! – resulting in a soaking wet carpet, very smelly; so to avoid this I put the bag and stand in a bowl on the floor to catch any drips. A simple enough procedure, one would think, but it is surprising the muddle some get into when doing it!

Another concern of mine is to maintain Sandie's oral health. Having a compromised and damaged immune system, anything going into the mouth and then into the alimentary tract, if not fully cooked or digested properly, or dealt with by this immune system, is a potential hazard to life.

So apart from body cleanliness, we have to have those systems open to the wide world constantly in mind. About a month ago she complained of toothache. Now Sandie is meticulous in cleaning her teeth, but she could tell me which tooth it was. It did not have any obvious cavity in it, but I noticed that her mouth was very dry and she seemed to have that first line of defence – saliva – in short supply. The dentist, when contacted, agreed to see her a week later at home and he did indeed find a cavity in a molar tooth and arranged to fill it in the near future. However, the following day – a Saturday, of course, when little help is available – she complained of even more pain, and when I inspected her mouth I found that she had a severe infection of thrush. Not an uncommon event in the life of the diabetic, but this was a first for her. I managed to get a tube of an oral anti-fungal preparation that morning, and by the Monday morning not only was the thrush clearing but her toothache had subsided. But she had obviously ingested some of the thrush and for a week or so afterwards had a mild gut upset with frequent bowel actions until treated systemically with an anti-fungal preparation.

There are so many things one has to keep an eye on with the chronically sick, as little things can get missed unless one looks at the big picture at all times. Even the smallest thing can spell trouble if you don't watch out. Again, it's the things they don't complain of you need to watch for. The patient may think the latest problem is of no concern, but when yesterday, Sandie, shaking her head and frowning, replying to my questioning said she had a frontal headache and 'always had a bit of pain around the catheter', I put her straight on the bed and looked at her leg bag which I found full of debris instead of the usual clear urine she passes. Headaches and cystitis go together. Fortunately, she had no infection, but a bladder washout soon cleared the trouble, which by evening would have been a major incident in her day.

And as for her hair – well, I let the hairdresser do that… unless I have to! The hairdresser says I do it reasonably well when I do have to wash and dry it! Unfortunately, I did not train as a hairdresser, but as a teacher of nursing and acupuncturist, not quite the same thing!

CHAPTER 20

HOPE

Hope, indeed, springs eternal as I have already observed in these writings.

When first diagnosed and treated, Sandie despaired of ever getting back to a normal life. She had to give up her job, was unfit to drive, could not dance or have the normal life that other young women of her age enjoyed. Even with the treatment available, and there was not a lot all those years ago, she just continued to deteriorate. She had lost control of her life, but did eventually find, with my help, an acceptable way of living. I must admit that I loved her from the moment she consulted me. My heart went out to this poor girl, but circumstances were such that we did not enter that perilous and treacherous world, and it was not until as you have read, many years later, we were able to enjoy the love we both felt for each other when first we met, now in changed circumstances, of course. Indeed, I loved many of my patients, even those who were unlovable. It would have required a very hard heart to not do so, as so many of my patients were refugees from conventional medicine and often despaired of finding somebody who would listen and pull out all the stops to help, and I pride myself in thinking that I never knowingly let anybody down.

But of the sufferers in despair of help with their problems, many I know have gone for quack cures, and I am well aware that I too was once referred to as a quack, until my therapy proved more successful than my accuser using conventional treatment experienced herself! All of my treatment was based upon a sound knowledge of physiology and modern medical treatments of the day. I say 'of the day' as things change so rapidly that it is sometimes difficult to keep up with progress made in care, unless one has enough time to read all the journals, enabling one not to give false hope, but an honest appraisal of the patient's condition. If still flummoxed by some of the things patients complain about, to seek more experienced and knowledgeable help, I have known people with severe neurological conditions try these special advertised treatments and diets, spend a lot of money and at times put their health or the chance of improvement at risk by doing so. But it is rather sad when somebody like me comes up with a simple answer which totally satisfies the sufferer, to have the orthodox practitioner laugh at it and destroy the patient's confidence by saying, "It's all in the mind." That may be so, but if he feels a benefit, and it does no harm, they should be glad to hear of such things and that somebody had done something to help.

I have also known of those who sought the help of a faith healer and did not get better either. Well, why should they? The pathology is that damage has been done to the physiology; only the body itself can cure that if the patient is using the correct treatment. A disease like, for example, pneumonia is the body's response to the pneumococcus bacterium. It is a natural thing for it to respond by consolidation of the lung and inflammation. The disease state is just that. Antibiotics do not cure pneumonia; they kill the bacteria causing the consolidation and inflammation of the lung, then the body's natural healing power steps in, and the cure – hopefully – is complete. No, faith healing will not cure the body, but will give a feeling of comfort and hope – both things the sufferer of an intractable condition needs, and the sense that somebody in whom you have confidence and concern will listen to your troubles. Harold Kushner, in his book *When bad things happen to good people*, comments that whoever you are and whatever your beliefs, you will respond the same way as all other persons to disease and trouble, and when the question "Why me?" is asked, he says, "Why not you, what is so special about you compared with somebody else?" The wicked suffer as much as the righteous: that's life. It's how you respond to illness that decides how much you will have to put up with. If you don't agree, go to the *Book of Job* in the *Old Testament*! 3,000 years of wisdom, and read what his hope was in and how he coped!

Sandie had all these fancy vitamins and other 'things'. The only thing they achieved was a substantial amount of money in the seller's bank balance. Little of it was of any value, but offered hope that she might get some relief from it all, but she did not, and it required a far more skilful approach than all of what these dubious practitioners offered. They were all the same: "Here, try these. They should help," and walked away to leave her in loneliness and with hope unfulfilled. Even in conventional medicine, it was the same.

In the '90s, cannabis was the buzzword that would help the pain of the spasms, she was told. "I only hope," so said she, but like a lot of other ideas it was not for her. Was there anything that would work to give relief, or just hope that tomorrow would be better than today, that she would have a better night tonight, that she would continue to have the courage to face another day? Rather a bleak prospect, you must agree. But they all treated her disease, not her.

But there have been remarkable results at times in the most extraordinary ways from those who do try and help, but do it for love, not for money or prestige…

When I was teaching nurses one afternoon, a student came to see me to ask if she would be allowed to go off duty early. She had a 'bad back' and looked quite tired and stressed. I had known of her problem and advised her to get medical help, but even after the prescribed physiotherapy, she had not improved. I subsequently learned when she recovered that she had an unhappy marriage and had recently had her son in trouble with the authorities. Also, she had lost her mother within the past year. "Who are you going to see?" I asked.

She looked at me nervously. "You won't laugh, will you? But he's a faith healer and I hope he can help me," she replied.

"No," I replied. "I won't laugh. Go and see what he can do for you and we will see you in class in the morning."

The next morning, a totally different girl came into the classroom. She no longer limped, she was smiling, all the stress seemed to have gone. "Come and talk with me at coffee break," I said. She came into my office and sat down. "So what happened?" I asked.

"I got to the church, the parish church," she began nervously. "I couldn't go in," she confessed. "You go to church; I don't. You're used to it," she burst out. I smiled encouragement. She continued hesitantly. "So I turned to go and the vicar came out. He was waiting for me in the porch. 'Come on,' he said. 'It's up to you. You don't have to if you don't want to; I'll wait inside.'" But she did go in and he invited her to come into the chancel and kneel down at the altar rails.

He then talked to her and, "I'm afraid I just spilled the beans. It all came tumbling out. I don't know if it was him or the building that did it, but I know I was exhausted and crying at the end. He asked me a few questions, then while I was still kneeling, he put his hands on my head and started to talk very quietly," she said.

"What did he say?" I asked.

"I don't know; it was as if he was just talking to a friend," she replied. She had been sitting in the chair in front of my desk, her head down, looking at her hands for about fifteen minutes as she told me this. Suddenly she looked up at me and burst out, "Then I got up with no pain or worries and walked out, and here I am, much better," she smiled.

Yes, she wanted to be heard, but did not know it! But somebody did, understood and listened, and wanted to! He took the time to understand and work it out for her. And that's the trick. Proper practitioners don't just prescribe and walk away! Having been one for many years, I know. Sometimes the most unlikely fact you can uncover takes the lid off and brings comfort and relief. Yes, it takes time and that needs good management skills. Time is always in short supply, but as a venerable and very caring retired doctor once said to me when I was overwhelmed with work, "Well, you'll have to make time to die!" A trite remark maybe, but true!

CHAPTER 21

SO WHO DOES THE PATIENT LOOK TO FOR CARE?

I am so glad that I am able to look after Sandie and meet both her needs and wants, but there are many who have companions who are not competent to do this, and they have to employ others to do the job. There are not enough people willing to do this task, as it requires so much commitment. In years past, the eldest daughter, or some other close relative, was expected to do this. Times change and we are living in a different world to the one in which I was brought up; our legislators do not as yet give a lot of thought to the increasing problem of the elderly – which is increasing year on year as the population ages – although they talk a lot about it! And according to photographs in the media, care of the elderly is usually presented as a circle of elderly people, all in wheelchairs or other seating arrangements, being conducted by some youngster singing songs or playing bingo. And so, if you will allow me, a few more thoughts on staff who are paid to provide care at home for those who are unable to look after themselves due to their illness or infirmity.

So far as management of time for care, in the case of somebody like Sandie, how long is a piece of string? She would, if alone, need at least four visits a day; the shortest, for example, might be twenty minutes (just to check all is o.k.), or up to one and a half hours for getting up and dressed. Toileting with the elderly cannot be rushed – ancient bowels do their own thing! If it is rushed, then, with no result at the time, an hour later the carer has to return to clear up the mess when the gut does decide to work, but then only if they have the time. If they have other commitments, they risk the patient getting pressure sores, which take even longer to attend to. Even proper mouth care can take a good five to ten minutes. Where in all this is the time to listen to the patient's concerns, or to comfort, or advise?

So far as cost is concerned, at present we both have a continuing income that is adequate for most things, but money can run out. £50 to £100 per day is about right for twenty-four hour care. It should be worth that if done properly. But if it is done, it needs to be done to an acceptable standard, and with the approval of the patient, so long as the patient knows what he wants, or if he does not, it must be decided by those who do know how to care. Otherwise it is about the same as factory farming!

Unfortunately there is of course no career structure for these people who by and large are well meaning, but know little or nothing about the immensity of task. So far as I am aware, having dealt with some groups, their staff training lasted two weeks on average, and was usually either office-based or classroom-based according to the 'industry standard', as the Care Quality Commission informed me. A certificate of completion of a course of training is not, I believe, issued. The testing on completion seems to be by the same people who trained them, so there is a chance their instructor may pass them fit for practice not having tested them in a real situation with real patients. So the carer can go out as quickly as possible to 'care' for the most vulnerable section of the community. There appears to be no accountability in the behaviour of the company or the employed apart from a moral one. I once questioned the people I contracted to care for Sandie, why they did not clean her properly; I was told they were not a nursing agency, but a caring one! I had made the mistake of observing that their employee was showing bad nursing practice when they did not wash the patient's bottom after a bowel action and before getting them dressed again! In my opinion there should at least be an entrance test concerning the ability of the candidate to understand the language, write in a legible way (to keep notes of certain occurrences), a basic understanding of hygiene and cleanliness, awareness of confidentiality and the obvious need to communicate, and then to enter the 'training course' as set by 'the industry'. If accepted, as it is a practical course, learn either on model independent patients – not on each other, but real ones – including a placement of, say, a week in a NHS geriatric unit at the end of their training. Then, with a certificate of competence, they should be accountable to a central body and placed on a register. They might then have more understanding about the care of the sick than I have found from some of them at present.

Were there a career structure, with a separate pay scale, this would encourage those who thought it a good idea at the time to 'have a go', to then realise they had some standing in the community which would appeal to their pride – never a bad thing! Call them Registered Domiciliary Carers, give them recognition! Let them put RDC after their name! Nurses and doctors are held in high regard in the community, why not carers?

So far as the individual caring for a relative at home is concerned, a short course could be offered to these carers, offering advice on what to look for in their charge's situation, and how to recognise even a minor change in the patient's medical condition. Instead of troubling the medical or nursing authorities with fatuous questions about the obvious, they would know when or when not to call for help. But they should always be supported, come what may; it's a lonely job caring for the sick on your own, and produces its own casualties.

CHAPTER 22

AND SO ON, AND ON, AND ON...! IT NEVER ENDS!

What will you wake up to? asks the headline in a magazine. Yes indeed, what?

"Oh, the usual things," we say, mainly without giving too much thought to the question or the questioner. "Same things as yesterday, probably." True maybe, but in the care of the sick it is never the same as yesterday, much similitude, indeed, but never without a variation upon a well-worn theme. It's all a matter of degree: some things better, some easier to accomplish, some worse, some enough to enrage you and some, when they turn out well, bring a smile to your face; not that you should ever not have a smile when dealing with your patient, hard though it is at times when you've been moaned at for something you didn't do because in the confusion you forgot, or you misunderstood the voice of pain which easily overwhelms sweet reason at times of stress Asking a colleague, a district nurse friend of mine, why she had given up her actor boyfriend, glamorous as he was, she told me that when she had had a bad day, her patient had died, another shouted at her, she dropped a sterile dressing on the floor, all this master of the thespians' art could tell her about his day was, "I've been doing breathing exercises today to learn how best to project my voice," whilst the only thing she'd dealt with that day which projected for her, was a child with an obstruction who vomited undigested food over her shoes! Yes, that's what it's all about in nursing the sick! But, for all that, there is certainly more variety in my life than in Sandie's.

We both view each day hopefully, not false hope that a cure for MS is just around the corner. We are both well aware that one day this will happen, but it's too late for Sandie. The damage of years is done. No, not false hope, but we do sometimes feel aggrieved at the billions spent on research on space travel and other most interesting things that have little bearing on our lives compared with the everlasting problems of finding enough money to care for the sick in all societies, whilst silly men continue to kill each other with more and more expensive methods which the taxpayer has to pay for, because some men do not like what their victims believe in! But of course, most of those who do this have no immediate health problems themselves, or their minds would work in another direction. But their day will come, as everybody is headed for the same situation – the grave. No, our hope is to get a better day today than yesterday by having learned the lessons of yesterday, and be determined not to repeat the mistakes of yesterday – today!

So for Sandie and I, the world goes by almost unnoticed by ourselves outside these four walls, apart from the intrusion of news bulletins on TV, and so on. Rarely do we get visitors, apart from our dear friend Pat who is always available for us night or day. May God bless that woman; she is a saint! Neither of us can visit the shops, nor have a meal out. We have the garden, a constant source of interest with the wildlife and plants, and we are always pleased to see anybody who can bring themselves to call and who are not worried that we might have something for them to do for us which may take some of their valuable time. There seems to be so little time available for most people nowadays. I know that I could often do with twenty-five hours in a day sometimes when Sandie nosedives for some reason, but this is our life, although I did not realise the complexity of life caring for the disabled before I married Sandie. I soon learned how to do it, and together we work well and have a reasonable existence, or should I say life, because we do have our own lives and that is together as one, and we hope as one. The world changes around us but we are stable and I know that but for the faith I have in the goodness of God, I could have given into despair at times – the opposite of hope!

But what of my Sandie? What does she think about it now, after all these years of trouble caused by this dreadful disease? She has limited cognitive skills left, but is well aware of all that is going on. Frankly, it would have broken my spirit had it been me, but she soldiers on with all the frustrations and depredations that life has thrown at her. Indeed, she has this deep well of misery into which she plunges when the going gets hard, but then gets out and puts the lid back on with a smile. I know that she does it so as not to affect me, but how she does it I don't know; but she does and this is the wonderful thing about her. Just how the human spirit can rise above it all and survive to fight another day is the wonder of being a human being. I know she is pleased with the methods of care I use to look after her and she knows it is done with love. How long can we go on like this? Well, how long is a piece of string? But the daily battle has to be fought for both of us and we look forward in reality to nothing more than more battles just the same, which up to now we have won each time, and with hope rather than despair. Our hope is that we can win, whatever happens and whatever life throws at us. Perhaps some clever person will come up with a better way for us. They do spend a lot of time debating and talking about it and that is usually as far as it gets. I do sometimes wonder if any of these debaters have MS themselves or have looked after a loved one with Sandie's problems. No, of course not; her problems are unique to her, but there is a similarity between all who are afflicted. Having cared for Sandie for all these years, with, I might add, my own problems of coronary heart disease, and with little acknowledgement or help offered, apart from when Sandie is too poorly and I ask for some minor thing to ease things along, I was warned a few weeks ago that if I did not attend for a blood test (admittedly after I'd received three blood forms to test my kidney function after twelve years on anti hypertensive drugs, and I had informed them of my transport difficulties and the problem of leaving my totally dependent wife on her own, or try and find someone to sit with her whilst I was away from the house, and telling the medical centre so by letter and two phone calls), I would have my treatment stopped for not conforming. This, for an administrative reason, made my blood boil, after all I had done for their patient – Sandie – over the years with minimal outside care – and so I threatened them with legal action claiming they would be in breach of a duty of care to me under the NHS Act 1946 if they persisted. Result

– silence! This hardly shows an awareness of the chronic patient and her eighty–five–year–old carer, does it? And now they talk of moving services into the community!

But lastly, yes, I am retired. No, I don't have to do this. The alternative is to have or buy the services of somebody else to do it, and then I have to sit by, watching that person doing things that I know Sandie does not like, or they do not have the competence to perform the required tasks correctly and she is too sweet to complain. But there are many relatives who have no choice, or finances, or the right circumstances to get help, and they may also have to look after children, or grandchildren, and/or husbands or wives, or have a job, and every day it gets harder, and then when the end comes for their loved one, along with the grief and the business of sorting out the mess, there is the guilt they feel that their chief emotion is sadly of sheer relief, often not spoken, but bottled up inside. And believe me, there are some like this. I met them when I was in practice: relatives distressed and guilty about their feeling of relief.

So I rest my case. Yes, there is more I could say and probably fill another book. There are many like us in this situation, but enough is enough, and if anybody finds my scribbling useful, I will be satisfied! I don't know if I am tilting at windmills too much, but when one is in the middle of it, responsible and somewhat lonely, you often think, *If only someone could come up with a better way of doing this!* So we soldier on, one day at a time. You can't rush it, step by step, as John Henry Newman said: *I do not wish to see the distant scene, one step enough for me.* That's it, one step at a time. And each day, when you've both got through it successfully again, a triumph; and that is what you have to be grateful for. The bad days? Learn from them and press on and smile; no good doing anything else! And when I see that quiet smile on Sandie's face, then I know it's all right… but let the Victorian poet John Oxenham have the last word in his poem *Road-Mates*:

Come share the road with me, my own

Through good and evil weather;

Two better speed than one alone,

So let us go together .

Come share the road with me, my own

You know I'll never fail you,

And doubts and fears of the unknown

Shall never more assail you

Come share the road with me, my own

I'll share your joys and sorrows.

And hand in hand we'll seek the throne

And God's great glad tomorrow

Come share the road with me, my own

And where the black clouds gather

I'll share thy load with thee my love,

And we'll press on together

And as we go we'll share also

With all who travel on it,

For all who share the road with me

Must share with all upon it

So make we – all one company

Love's golden cord our tether,

And, come what may, we'll climb the way

Together – aye together!

Don Snuggs B.E.M. S.R.N. R.C.N.T. Lic Ac. March 20i7